PRAISE FOR WE'R
HO~~CKE~~~~Y~~

L. Zukosky uses humor and wit to chronicle the parents' journey of dreaming their child could be "the next one." This book is a must-read for parents who have lost sight of whose dream they are living and for gullible parents with a blank cheque just entering the hockey world. Her self-deprecating humor, real-life experiences and observations expose the lunacy of youth hockey. It's an indispensable guide to parents of the next generation.

— JUSTIN DAVIS, BESTSELLING AUTHOR OF *CONFLICTED SCARS: AN AVERAGE PLAYER'S JOURNEY TO THE NHL.*

Having 5 hockey players of my own, This book hit home with the passion, drive and determination that it takes to pursue a dream in sports along with the struggles, sacrifices and perseverance that is takes to achieve it! Laura's recount of the years spent was both funny and yet serious. I want to thank her for this memoir of the years that our sons played together! Thanks for the Mints!

— WENDI "MAMA SLAVS" SLAVIN, HOCKEY MOM.

As the founder of an all female, work from home team, I know a thing or two about busy mom life & the pressures we put on ourselves to nurture our kids' ambitions (often sacrificing our own). But I cannot say I could put myself in the shoes of a hockey parent without reading 'We're not here for the hockey.'

Laura's book took me through all the emotions of parenting. The highs of acceptance and wins; the lows of uncertainty and loss. I thoroughly enjoyed this through the lens of a sister to a hockey sibling (wow do I appreciate what my parents did!) and now the lens of a parent (with children currently too young for year round sports). Laura's book is a masterclass in parenting, life, life as a sports parent and how to just be a good human being. Her navigation tips are the perfect touch of actionable advice in a delightfully entertaining life story.

I love her ability to paint a big dynamic picture then bring you down into a simple moment that allows you to experience just what she went through. Sometimes joyful, other times anxiety provoking. But almost always funny (she's really funny).

This is also a story about family, community and having one another's back. I particularly appreciate the challenges hockey would bring to couples to fairly divide the invisible labor and mental load that goes into years of sports participation. Millions of couples work to find fairness over simply doing the dishes.

I love Laura's recounts and life lessons...and I secretly want to join her for a parent fandango. I'd highly recommend this entertaining read for sports parents and parents alike. Bravo, Laura!

— Emily A. Hay, Founder & CEO, Hay There Social Media; As Seen In the Fair Play Documentary, produced by Reese Witherspoon's Hello Sunshine, directed by Jennifer Siebel Newsom, based off Eve Rodsky's NYTimes best selling book.

I found this story to accurately represent a thoughtful, humorous journey into competitive sports and ice hockey. As a parent of a former women's gymnastics "rising star," I could relate to the emotional roller coaster of the experiences, the impact on the family dynamics, the time and sacrifice of travel, and the financial tolls of the success of my child. I highly recommend this read!

— CORI COSTELLO PH.D., LCMHCS, LCPC, ATR-BC, ATCS.

When I picked up this book, I didn't know a stick from a puck (I don't come from a big sports family, and my kid is an actor, not an athlete), so I was astonished by how much I related to the experiences L. Zukosky describes in this hilariously helpful guide to staying sane while raising a competitive kid. If you've ever asked yourself, "Is it really worth all this?" only to see the smile on your child's face and realize that question has just answered itself, this is the book for you!

— DR. ADRIENNE MACIAIN, BESTSELLING AUTHOR OF SPARK GENIUS: CREATIVE FLOW UNLEASHED.

WE'RE NOT HERE FOR THE HOCKEY

A GUIDE TO RAISING A COMPETITIVE
ATHLETE (WITHOUT GOING NUCKING FUTS)

L. ZUKOSKY

Red Thread Publishing LLC. 2023

Write to **info@redthreadbooks.com** if you are interested in publishing with Red Thread Publishing. Learn more about publications or foreign rights acquisitions of our catalog of books: www.redthreadbooks.com

Paperback ISBN: 978-1-955683-55-5

Ebook ISBN: 978-1-955683-56-2

Cover Design: The Ideas Factory, Karla Mira **theideasfactory.com.co**

CONTENTS

IN MEMORY OF COACH SERGEI BAUTIN

(1967-2023)

A NOTE FROM THE AUTHOR

This is a book of memory, and memory has it's own story to tell. It is about my voyage through the world of hockey and the people I met along the way. It is all as seen through my eyes and reflects my experience. I have changed the names of people I encountered in this world but all of them were doing their best in their own way to promote this wonderful sport. I have done my best to make it tell a truthful story.

Dedication

To my family
To my friends
To my hockey family
To the coaches
To the youth hockey organizations
To the teachers
To the trainers
To the physical therapists, doctors and dentists
To the staffs at team hotels
To the rental van agencies
To the bus drivers
To the volunteers at tournaments
To the airlines that never lost our sticks
To the Zamboni drivers
To the Refs
To the skate sharpening guys
To the hockey store guys
To the staff at food chains, Italian restaurants, food delivery, and big
box stores
To the Haircutters
May we always remember that kindness matters. Thank you.

INTRODUCTION

I'll never forget the day I picked up my son from a three-day "intensive" hockey program. He was 11 years old. The coach recommended I register my son for the fall tryouts in their AAA hockey program. The coach believed he had the potential to be an "elite" hockey player. Who was I to get in the way?

Naive, hopeful, and happy to support my child's desire to compete at a higher level than the YMCA Rec league, I signed the first check for $6,000 after he made the team. This initial investment was a down payment for a plot of uninhabited land, a diversion of funds intended for a college savings account or perhaps a mythical portfolio of Bitcoin and GameStop. The actual financial investment, over the next 6 years, brought forth a lifetime of stories, the need to side-hustle for cash, character building, and absolute mayhem and fun.

So why this book?

We're not here for the hockey. That's only part of the story.

Our role is akin to a mountain guide who accompanies a climber for the trek to the summit.

This book is a field guide to navigating the family journey of competitive athletics. My story is about hockey, but your story could be about baseball, soccer, gymnastics, or any sport that takes over your weekends. This book is a compilation of awkward situations, fruitful mistakes, truth bombs, and constructive criticism for the imperfect "system."

As my son's hockey sherpa, I set up camp, cooked the food, and schlepped the heavy gear of emotional and financial stress so that my son could focus on his dream, the game, the team, schoolwork, and being a good kid. I wore flip-flops up the mountain without a planned route and valued camaraderie, all the while accepting payment in the form of gratitude and a good winter jacket for the rink. There were storms, missed turns, predators, and plenty of crazy days on the trek, but I wouldn't trade it for the world.

Let's meet at base camp. Here are a few navigational tips from someone who's been in the weeds to get you started:

1. Never mix beer, wine and/or hard liquor the night before an early game.
2. Pack Pedialyte packets, Tylenol and ibuprofen as recovery from The Parent Fandango (see chapter 7).
3. Leave your debit card at home, unless you're really good at gambling.
4. Skip the Frappuccino; you'll gain the Freshman 15 again. Stick with black coffee.
5. Always have gum or mints for the friend who sits next to you on the bleachers. They forget, and one of you has bad breath.
6. Carry Band-aids, extra layers, gloves, a packable blanket, and an insurance card.
7. Don't underestimate the power of lucky jackets, lucky purses, lucky hats, lucky seats, or the text to the Italian grandmother to pray to St. Anthony. They all matter; hockey fans are superstitious.
8. Convert to Buddhism. Okay, unrealistic. But anytime something really pisses you off, just W.A.I.T. (translation: Why Am I Talking?). Following this rule is paramount to your kid's chances of getting to the next level, and to your

chances of being considered anything other than the team asshole.

9. Don't post on social media, unless it's a team photo from a Championship game. We get it, you're proud. Text the personal stuff to Paw-paw and Mee-maw, and spare everyone else's feed.

10. No ranting. It's not a good look, and you can never take it back. Seriously, more to come later on shutting the hole in the middle of your face for a lot of stuff that goes down. There is a time and a place and it's never in public.

11. Train your player to avoid posting on social media unless they have a professional proofreader on staff. It's a jungle out there. Plus there's a good chance they'll need a real job someday.

So, your kid wants to play their sport at a high level. Great! They'll need to work hard, have heaps of fun, build friendships, and hone in by the age of 12. They have their own path and plenty of obstacles to overcome. This book scratches the surface of what is ahead. Spoiler alert: it is equal parts euphoric, action-packed, and crazy-making. Prepare yourself in advance for the "not so fun" parts: politics, favoritism, injustice, injury, greed, bad genetics, and dumb luck.

This book is not about what it takes for a kid to "make it" at a high level in hockey, or any sport for that matter. There are a million ways things could turn out based on where you live, who you know and if the kid has the right amount of talent (and resources) to earn a spot on the next team.

Instead, I am speaking directly to your inner voice. You know, the one that started chattering away the moment your kid got their first invite to an *elite* tournament. It's a visceral emotion; hits you right in the solar plexus. An intuitive spark electrifies the vein supplying blood to your brain. This paves a pathway for consumption of the gateway drug to pay-check sports. Ingredients include: organic pride, exclusivity, excitement, and gluten-free fear. CAUTION: may contain nuts. And the more you consume it, the more nuts you're likely to encounter. "My kid is special and someone else noticed!" Just a taste, a small toke of the joint, a hit that possesses the pen in your hand to write the check and reign in compulsive behavior. The kid is really good at something and loves it. And you love your kid.

And just like that: you're hooked.

Load up the pack, strap on the gear: we're heading up.

1

THE SPORT EMBRYO

Asport picking a kid happens in different ways. Maybe a parent played semi-pro or pro, an older sibling or cousin played in college, you live in a hockey-focused region, or the kid just tried something new and landed a Championship title in their hometown.

Navigation Tip: Some quantum physics is involved when your kid goes from trying a new sport to becoming obsessed. Only if they (NOT you) are obsessed, is it a good idea to start saving money for the travel funds. Start small, don't get the "best" of everything. Make them work for it. It builds character and reduces your chances of raising an entitled jerk.

At the age of 10, my son decided to play hockey. Too late, in the opinion of every hockey coach.

We had moved to Colorado from Chicago, and the Stanley Cup playoffs were in full swing. The Chicago Blackhawks were magical, not the biggest or most physical team, but wicked fast and extraordinarily skilled. The year was 2010, and after coming up short in the 2009 playoffs, the Blackhawks picked off their competition one game at a time.

Our family had assigned seats on the couch: who was in the room at the time of a goal demanded that all things must be repeated, otherwise it would be our fault if they lost. It all came down to us: we felt a connection to all the Chicago Blackhawks fans on the planet. We talked directly to the TV so that Patrick Kane, Jonathan Toews, Marian Hossa and Duncan Keith could hear us. We told them when they did something stupid and applauded them for their perfectly executed plays. We idolized Coach Q, with his stone face expression and austere façade. Aside from the Chicago Cubs, this team needed to claim the Championship holy grail after a long drought. The White Sox World Series win was old news; Blackhawk fans pooled their collective juju between beer runs and beef sandwiches and we made it happen. You're welcome, Chicago Blackhawks! You couldn't have done it without this new Colorado family rooting for you from our couch.

My son was mesmerized. He teared up if they lost. He put on roller blades and did victory laps in our cul-de-sac anytime the Hawks won a game. I bought him a used, extra-small women's cut Patrick Kane jersey off of eBay. He wanted to play hockey, but we told him it was an only-child sport, and being one of four kids, there was no way this was going to be in his future. We dismissed it, hoping he'd get bored or distracted. Didn't he know that people who played hockey had backyard ice rinks? We lived too close to the sun in Colorado, our pond ice melted by noon.

We noticed he was slowly slipping into obsession. It started with him watching highlight reels on ESPN. He memorized playoff schedules, then found YouTube videos on famous hockey players in Canada, Russia, Sweden, Finland and the US. He wanted to watch any live hockey game on TV, so we bought him a knee hockey set from Walmart, hoping to quell his desire. We encouraged him to simply follow in the footsteps of his brothers and play baseball and soccer. Ho Ho Ho...How about a nice football for Christmas?

We had ski passes for 6 people that winter; there was no room for a sport that directly conflicted with our winter plans. This is why we moved out of the Midwest for Christ's sake! We were tired of long, miserable winters spent indoors, driving in ice storms, ridiculous taxes, and chubby kids on the couch playing videogames. My husband and I were trying to cheat an early death and avoid high cholesterol and Type II diabetes, so we headed for the hills. Literally. No more dad coaches, traffic jams and obligatory birthday parties at Chuck-E-Cheese. We had plans. Plans that included hiking, mountain biking, skiing, camping, and fishing. I envisioned an L.L. Bean magazine life: cute wool hats, sipping hot chocolate against a breathtaking mountain backdrop, all cuddled up with our goldendoodle labs, telling scary-as-shit ghost stories while staring at a campfire.

Spoiler alert: this fantasy never materialized.

Except for the dogs, and they weren't goldendoodlabs but rescue mutts from the Humane Society. They deserved a shot at suburban life after all they'd been through.

In the final Stanley Cup game of 2010, my wide-eyed son, with his extra-small women's cut Patrick Kane jersey, sat on the couch watching Game 6 against the Philadelphia Flyers (who were also on a long-awaited quest to win the Cup). The game went into overtime and we had exhausted our superstitions. I believe at some point someone had moved slightly to the edge of their seat and we all simultaneously yelled at them as if they had murdered the family dog. The hockey beast in all of us had been summoned, and it was out for blood. If anyone had walked in the door or called us on the phone, we could have shot them in the head. Nobody better be asking me to buy school project trifolds tonight, or I'm gonna lose it. There was no room for chit-chat, distraction, bathroom breaks, extra movement, or breathing. We had to do our part and hold down the fort so that Patrick Kane could score the Game Winning Goal (GWG) to clinch the Cup. Only Kane and our Colorado family knew that the puck went in, even the announcers weren't sure, so we had to take the celly for him until the rest of the world caught up with what had just happened.

〜

Non-hockey people tip: it may be obvious to hockey, but others need to know that a celly *is when a hockey player celebrates a goal.*

We all reveled in the celebration, cried when the older players hoisted the cup, and pranced around the room while the dogs barked at us.

We went outside. No fireworks in forest-fire-prone Colorado, but we imagined it. However, in our cul-de-sac there were plenty of refugees from the Midwest to join us in our celebration. Even the St. Louis Blues fans came out to reluctantly congratulate us. One of the houses filled with Chicago fans spilled out onto the sidewalk after gorging on the Portillo's hot dogs and beef sandwiches they had shipped in. Everyone was celebrating and lamenting that we weren't in Chicago with our childhood friends for this event. The cool thing about being a crazy Chicago fan (Bears, Blackhawks, Bulls, Cubs, White Sox) is that there is an instant bond. You could be a complete asshole and a fellow Chicagoan will hug and high-five you when anything good happens with one of those teams. Sports kinship.

Meanwhile, our son skated at full speed around the cul-de-sac on his rollerblades, wearing his extra-small women's cut Patrick Kane jersey. Never once did I worry that he wasn't wearing a helmet or knee pads. In that moment, he was invincible.

That summer was the quintessential Colorado vacation. Our older two boys liked to ride dirt-bikes so we packed up our Honda Pilot with coolers, junk food, and camping equipment and towed our newly purchased pop-up camper into the wilderness. The soon-to-be hockey player did not have a dirt bike, so he used a tree branch to stick handle some rocks. After a few days of living off of Oreos and Lucky Charms, we came home and thought about the rest of summer in Colorado. Little did we know that 5 years later we would have to sell those bikes and that pop-up camper to pay for hockey.

Cue up Alanis Morissette's song, *Ironic*: "It's the good advice that you just didn't take and who would've thought....it figures." That's some good Canadian guru shit.

I decided to sign him up for a "learn-to-play" hockey camp at the local YMCA. He had turned 10 years old in May and he needed something to do before school started in August. I took him skating a few times to the public skating sessions so he could try out his used hockey skates we had purchased from Play-It-Again Sports. He held onto the walls, looking like Rick Moranis as "Dark Helmet" from SpaceBalls, circa 1987. Hilarious. And so...damn...cute.

Since this was just a filler week before school started, it seemed like a great idea to give hockey a try. The first camp was sponsored by Planet Hockey, the instructors were cute young guys whose business was to introduce the kids to the sport. My husband assembled a bunch of items from Play-It-Again Sports, some lost-and-found elbow pads from the YMCA, and an old Sherwood stick that somehow ended up in our garage from a yard sale. I registered him at the reception table, they gave him a jersey and off he went!

Kids at the camp were all different ages. He was put in a group where most of the kids could already skate so I immediately thought he would hate it. I watched him try to keep up. He was a pretty athletic kid from a few years of playing soccer and baseball, and he was determined. After about one hour, they circled to center ice for a quick pep talk and I could see it in his eyes: he was hooked.

Back home, he immediately put on his roller blades, and skated full speed around the cul-de-sac. No helmet, no pads. Again. Very '80's of me because, when it comes to getting hurt, I take an old school attitude: you need a couple of good road rashes to motivate you to avoid them. As my father always said, it builds character. Rub some dirt in it, you're fine. My kid seemed to be improving, and I was happy he wasn't sitting on the couch playing video games. At that point in time, my entire goal in life was to keep my kids active so they'd be too tired to fight with each other.

The next few days at the camp, I watched him working hard to keep up with the real hockey players in the group. Money well spent! He seemed to be able to skate *and* hold a stick. At the same time! He was even batting the puck around like the other kids. At the end of the camp, one of the instructors handed him an extra medal from an old hockey tournament, and told him he had hockey smarts. I had no idea what that meant, but I took him home and got him ready for soccer practice.

He begged me to let him join the hockey team at the local YMCA; they were holding tryouts for their Squirt teams that October. I had no idea how I was going to find time to squeeze in another activity for my kids. Over-scheduling was inevitable in a family with 4 kids. I wished we lived on a farm with chickens and cows because they would be physically fit and off of their phones. But sadly, we lived in the 'burbs with only a few daily chores, not enough to keep everyone busy. The oldest brother was playing high school soccer, the next brother was playing middle school football, and the younger sister was involved in gymnastics. And he wanted to do *two* sports?? Holy hell.

Then again, I was already committed to hours of driving kids to activities (in addition to being the default for grocery shopping, laundry, paying bills, teaching fitness, and a futile effort on getting my own career on some type of trajectory other than full time chauffeur). What's a few more?

My husband took him to the tryout; he was coming in as a second-year Squirt. I had no idea what Squirt or Pee-Wee or Bantam or Midget meant. I thought it all sounded ridiculous and childish. How could these be actual terms used in an actual sport? I grew up watching the Chicago Blackhawks in the National Hockey League (NHL). I didn't know any hockey players in school despite having a huge crush on Eddie Olczyk as a teenager. Eddie was never a Pee-Wee or Midget! This must be a new thing. When they returned, my husband announced that our son had made the Squirt A team. Apparently he seemed to have some raw potential, and more importantly, they didn't have enough kids for a Squirt B team, so that was it! Make way for the participation ribbons!

About $200 later and a meeting about practices and games, it was off to the races between soccer and hockey dual (and at times, dueling) commitments.

The best thing about the YMCA is that they serve the community at-large, so sports are affordable. Also, the ice rink was 5 minutes from our house. That said, our two practices each week would be shared with 3 other teams, so 18 kids on a quarter sheet of ice plus 2 or 3 coaches was definitely "small area games" by the definition used in the American Development Model (ADM) for USA Hockey.

The main coach, Ricky, was THE guy who helped our son fall in love with the game of hockey. He was from a large family in Minnesota who grew up playing pond hockey with his friends and brothers. He played Minnesota high school hockey, and had three kids of his own, one of which played defense on the team he was coaching. He was a kick-ass coach, period. He really just loved hockey and his personality was such that he wanted to spend time with his youngest son to prepare him for the hockey beer league someday. Ricky played in college, had a hard shot, and was easy on the eyes. He owned a local business, took his family to Grand Lake on their boat and oftentimes talked about fishing. Nice guy.

Ricky asked my son to come a little early to practice with another kid to practice face-offs. It appeared that my kid had enough hand-eye coordination to pull it off, so we drove him to get the extra coaching. It was free. After a few practices, they played their first game and the kid seemed to really thrive. Ricky helped him fix his ankle bending problems by bringing in some shims for his skates, which seemed to help strengthen his ankles and help his skating. He also helped him with his stickhandling and called him Mr. Dangles after a few weeks.

One month in, he had a nickname.

There were two other coaches with sons on the team who volunteered to help our Squirt A team. One of them was called the Farter. This guy loved to purposely pass gas in front of the kids in line who were waiting their turn for a drill. Apparently the farts smelled like salami and aftershave, so my kid learned to hang back a few feet until the coach told him to go, giving new meaning to the explosive start. The other guy was an odd duck, but his son was a good player who liked to brag about how he would score all the goals and was the best kid on the ice. That kid is now a scratch golfer.

We had a few local tournaments and a fun excursion to Breckenridge where the kids went sledding up and down a huge hill right before the game. Parents seemed unconcerned about fatigue but Ricky recommended that kids shouldn't swim after 6 pm the day before a game. The kids could not wait to jump in the hotel pool when the tournament was over, it was their big prize to cannonball into the water and swim until they were pruned. The little skinny bodies would emerge from the pool, asking for buffalo wings or burgers that night.

I remember taking a few of the boys home and hearing how they all wanted to play in the NHL. In between talking about cartoons and their favorite part about recess in school, they were building their brotherhood. The kids who were part of the YMCA team had parents who still believed in skiing on the weekends, having a normal life, and even opted out of games if they conflicted with church or a birthday party. Missing a tournament was not out of the question either, coaches seemed to roll their eyes but did not bench anyone because of principled parents. This conversation always centered around finding a balance.

Fast forward 3 years, I would long for balance. Keep the faith but just know: the system is not set up for balance if your kid is passionate about their sport. Your Christmas decorations will be up until June. Home cooked meals? Start browsing for "hockey family meal hacks" and find support groups on Facebook. You get the point.

It was a fun season, and it was clear that my son really enjoyed this sport. We bought him a hockey net so he could practice shooting. Every day he would drag it to the end of our driveway while wearing his roller blades. I would picture Scooby Doo running in place with the Bongo-Run sound effect. Didn't have the heart to tell him to set up the net first, then put on the skates. He'd figure it out, plus it made me giggle. He would get a lacrosse ball and stick handle it while skating around the cul-de-sac, coming around with an errant shot that would end up in the neighbor's lawn, in the bushes or occasionally snatched by an off-leash dog. After work, my husband would put on some second-hand goalie pads he found at a yard sale and try to block shots. My older son would do the same and, if desperate enough, the little sister (age 7), would don the giant mask and pads and be goalie. Being the youngest of 4, you are told what to do. As the only girl, she had the reputation of *Princess Pitbull*, because she could turn on you if you pissed her off, all the while maintaining her adorable innocence. It made her a really good goalie.

When it was time to sign up for soccer again, my son asked to play hockey. Seriously, kid, we told you this is an only-child sport. We are short in stature, shorties don't make it (tell that to Jonny Gaudreau, Alex DeBrincat, Brad Marchand, or Cole Caufield). We could see that he was more serious about hockey, as we rarely found him kicking a soccer ball or watching soccer on TV.

He was all-in, reciting Chicago Blackhawks players by name and number. He memorized their stats, their country of origin, their college, and their trades, some real savant syndrome shit that may translate to winning Jeopardy someday. We thought it was cute and signed him up for another year at the YMCA. Why not? It was 5 minutes away and he seemed to be really interested in the sport.

We enabled his obsession by buying him all things Chicago Blackhawks for birthdays and Christmas. He had 2 Kane Jerseys, but his favorite players expanded to Marian Hossa, Jonathan Toews and Duncan Keith. Eventually he had a Patrick Sharp hat, a Brandon Saad T-shirt and a few more free promotional things that were given to me by a fellow fitness instructor whose uncle worked at the United Center. We had so many blankets and bobble heads, scarves and lunch boxes, hats and XXL T-shirts, we looked like we robbed the Blackhawks store. The godparents from Illinois sent my son a subscription for a Chicago Blackhawks train set which, every year, gifted him a new Lionel train car that will someday be collectors items. Good thing we never had to sell those to pay for hockey....I wonder how much they're worth? Asking for a friend.

Over the summer, we registered him for a couple of local hockey camps in between soccer and camping trips. Metaphorically speaking, one hockey camp is like planting a juniper plant in your front yard. The first camp starts out as a way to cover a few weeks of inactivity in the summer, but if you give them sunshine and some good soil, they will double or triple in size in a short amount of time. Add another camp, add another juniper plant. Their root system grows horizontally, sometimes 10 feet from the center, and they will eventually kill off any nearby plants. In case you haven't deciphered the metaphor, the juniper plant is hockey. As a kid gets older, the ability to play any other sport besides hockey becomes impossible, despite what all of the articles and hockey podcasts tell you. By the age of 12, you'd better decide what route you're going with this sport, since you will dedicate your time and money to it year-round.

Alas, still no pressure from us other than it was time for new skates. My husband brought him back to Play-it-Again Sports where he was able to sell back his previously used skates and purchased a new (used) pair for about $40. According to the salesman, this was a great deal. Can you imagine what a new pair of skates actually costs? *One pair of decent skates is about the cost of a new refrigerator, or maybe you'll need a Segway because your car was repossessed.* They found him a new stick for about $30 and different elbow pads because the ones we had borrowed from the lost-and-found should be put back after using them all season long.

We were amateurs, completely naive to where all this was going.

We questioned going back to the YMCA for his first Pee-Wee year after noticing that his skating had drastically improved. He was no longer hanging onto the walls and somehow had learned to stickhandle fairly well. We suggested checking out the local hockey club, a program that was considered a step up from the Rec league at the YMCA. But he didn't want to go. He'd made friends at the Y, and wanted Ricky for a coach again.

It was a really fun group of kids and parents and we liked how casual it was. I remember the set of twins on the team who were national champion skiers. They were really fast skaters, using hockey as cross-training while they collected sponsorships. They missed a bunch of practices and games because they were busy winning alpine skiing competitions. My son befriended them, admiring their ability to speak Spanish fluently while their little pale-skinned, freckled faces stunned anyone at a Mexican restaurant. He said that skating with the twins made him faster. He loved their competitive drive.

We had also become good friends with a family from Poland. Their son had a fantastic hockey setup in his basement, so my son would beg to go to their house to play. We went skiing a few times with their family, always getting a kick out of the never-ending supply of smoked sausages they'd keep in their pockets as snacks for the ski lifts. I could never resist asking "is that a sausage in your pocket or are you happy to see me?" My kids shunned me immediately, saying "Mom, you're disgusting." And of course I did it every time they offered me another sausage, maybe ending with a "that's what she said" to really fire them up. The father grew up playing pond hockey in Poland, he said it was a great escape from the stress before the fall of communism. He emigrated to the United States to get a good education, he had hoped his son would love hockey as much as he did growing up. He also mentioned getting good grades would be his son's first priority.

Before the Pee Wee tryouts, Ricky had partnered with a few other hockey coaches and created an "elite" hockey tournament, inviting our son to participate. Looking back, it was a quick way to assemble some pre-season games with local kids. For $180, you got a jersey and played for the team against other local teams who were also considered "elite." Putting the word "elite" in front of any parent who thinks their kid is somewhat talented is the ultimate ego-bait. We had no idea that it was a mild money grab; we just saw the word "elite" and lost a part of our soul to hockey.

Remember: juniper plant. The roots start to go a little deeper, away from the center of the plant, killing anything else around it. So, we paid up and let him play, only to watch the other "elite" club kick our ass 13-0. I don't think our club was anything more than a bunch of kids from the YMCA who had no ability to play hockey as a team. Every player tried to take it coast to coast. The other team was able to pass the puck a few times, which really faked our kids out. Passing the puck was something Squirts learned but had not mastered, so this concept blew their minds. We took our son home and he told us he needed to practice more.

The next season in Pee Wee was not great. A few kids didn't come back and then something shifted with the dad coaches. The main coach, Ricky, allowed the assistant coaches to make more decisions. He was starting a new business and wasn't trying to prop up his kid's NHL career. We started to notice how the other coaches' sons were getting to play longer shifts and the rest of the lines were either being skipped or changed around to accommodate the New World Order. I was sure *these* dad coaches were telling themselves they were being fair, they may have even professed it after the game in their own walk of shame. Our son was consistently working on the game of hockey, which Ricky continuously helped him refine either on the bench or in practice. However, if Ricky was unable to coach a game, it was obvious that the other two guys were ready to pounce and keep their kids out on the ice for double, even triple shifts. Every Power Play. Every Penalty Kill. Classic "he who holds the gold makes the rules." Our son was put on a line with a player who could barely stand up, let alone shoot the puck. The other kid on the line had no true interest in hockey and was always frustrated.

The YMCA needed volunteers to function, so you really have no case for getting fired up about nepotism. Talk about a first-world problem. Plus, according to my husband who had played team sports growing up, you cannot break the unwritten sports code and speak up about these matters. Unless someone is molesting your son, you really have nothing to say, because it is all part of "facing adversity" and "leaving it all on the ice." *Get used to hearing these two sayings from every higher level hockey coach. And a one, and a two, this time with more feeling!* As a result, my son decided that when he got older, he would set up a team with the tagline, "Don't sign up unless your kid is really into it." Brilliant.

The YMCA vibe is one that represents America at its best, a nostalgic trip down all things a kid loves. You know that excitement when your 2nd grader wants to set up their own lemonade stand? In their minds, they're creating a solid business plan by making the poster, deciding on the price, and finally setting up a table with cups and a pitcher of over-sweetened lemon-flavored drink. As they wave down the passersby, they are looking to make eye contact with the lone man walking his dog, the mom in the minivan coming home with groceries, the city worker in the pickup truck who must be thirsty. In that kid's mind, they have what that person needs and is unapologetic for the up-charge to make a profit on their parent's assets. It's that: a feeling of excitement of doing something awesome, executing a plan and living out their dream. Extra fun if their business partners are friends and pizza comes after the game.

The YMCA has the goods, and the kids feel like they are professional hockey players. A disco ball intended for the public all-skates at night would sometimes be turned on while a recording of the national anthem played excruciatingly loud. People stand up, men remove their hats, some place their hand over their heart. The sound of water bottles falling through the bleachers, the kids who are still talking to their friends, people pivoting left and right looking for where the actual American flag is in the place. Eventually all the fidgets are out by the time the lyrics get to "and the rockets red glare." It is in that moment, at that time, that nobody cares who is President, no mention of un-winnable or secret wars. Just a ritual where everyone knows that, as part of the social contract, we stand in unity and salute our flag. Regardless of how you feel about the U.S. or what you stand for, the kids on the ice are lined up to play a hockey game. They don't care about society, politics, or belief systems. The ones who have the dream to go all the way into the NHL may have hijacked a few moves of their favorite player, maybe shuffling their feet forward and back looking up at their parents who are smiling down at them hoping they are going to have fun and enjoy the game. Wouldn't it be great to get our national politicians to see what the local YMCA does for patriotism?

All of the games in the not-so-serious YMCA Rec league are, for the most part, forgettable. What may have seemed like an amazing play by your kid is quickly replaced with a really crappy decision that turned over the puck. Parents cheer, make "oooh" and "ahhh" sounds, shout out sayings like "ICE IT" or "c'mon ref" or "that's okay Jimmy" or "skate skate skate" or "shoot it!!!!" If an alien landed down and watched the mumblings of Pee Wee hockey fans, the Earthlings would be labeled as reactive lemmings. We sounded ridiculous with our incoherent bursts, chants and cheers looking for warmth under a track heater, sipping coffee, clapping our gloved hands or stomping our feet. I can't imagine we had any complete sentences until the end of a game. "They really played well as a team today," or "I don't know if they understand the rules, oh well."

After the game, the kids act as if nothing happened. Their sweaty wet heads, boogery noses and Gatorade stained tongues said it all. They were just kids, looking forward to hanging out with their teammates for a pizza party. Some families dip out to attend another kid's soccer game, while others wait around to see "who's all going." Kids immediately run outside asking if they can ride with the other kid in their car, and if they can have a sleepover, because 90% of all of our games were on Saturdays. Remember: two practices a week, one game on the weekends, maybe 2 or 3 tournaments the entire season. Easy peasy. Across the country, other hockey parents were already getting ulcers from taking the game way too seriously; searching for live-in coaches trying to emigrate, buying video analysis software, and considering heart meds. We were YMCA people. We were not *those parents*.

The hockey collective at this stage of the game was "a friendly game of hockey." It was fun to watch, cheer and notice that your kid was maybe picking up new skills and making friends. What I noticed, however, was that my kid was taking it more seriously than most of his teammates. He had the "magic mitts" as one kid said when he asked to borrow his gloves, thinking that would give him better hands. Now, I know what you're thinking: here we go, another mom with hockey-parent-syndrome, believing her kid's the best. But I really couldn't have cared less. I would brush off the parental compliments the way any parent would, just giggle knowing that my son had a bit of OCD.

As a younger kid, I would catch him throwing a tennis ball at the wall to try and catch it with the other hand. He would line up his Hot Wheels cars by size and sort them by color. He would stack his foreign coins by country and amounts, sort rocks and arrowheads such that they were symmetrically distant as if they were on display for purchase. He is left-handed, so the theory is that both sides of the brain are always working in tandem much less than the right-handed Cro-Magnon like the rest of us. I never thought much about it, third sons are always trying to "catch up" to the speed or strength of the older brothers. He had to find his own thing to control in order to soothe his otherwise competitive nature that he could never beat his brothers at anything (so they all thought).

Our last tournament of the Pee Wee season was in Taos, New Mexico. Our team still traveled with parents and everyone was on their own as to where to stay. The parents didn't really hang out much; we really didn't know half the families since their kids didn't play in every game. We found ourselves saying, "does anyone recognize #17 out there?" and have to ask around if anyone knew who their dad was in the group. We had a great time nonetheless, staying at an old hotel with the name Sagebrush in it, complete with an awesome homemade breakfast with biscuits and gravy and some really excellent Southwest dinners at a setting that looked like Tatooinie from Star Wars.

The team actually won that tournament with the game-winning goal by the player who couldn't stand up, with a beautiful spoon-fed pass by my kid. That one stuck in my head.

At the end-of-year party, I bought a set of Minnesota Wild beer mugs for Ricky and told him that we were ready to move on to another team. He seemed mildly sad but understood that Mr. Dangles was getting serious about playing more competitively.

~

Navigation Tip: The first hockey coach can make or break a kid's love for a sport. Ricky loved the sport so much that he conveyed his passion directly to how he coached. His calm mannerism, funny sense of humor, and Minnesota hockey prowess translated to my kid like a genetic chromosome.

Hockey and competition did not come from us. I played Badminton in high school and was a cheerleader like in the 1986 sports comedy movie Wildcats (U-G-L-Y, you ain't got no alibi - you Ugly- What What You Ugly); my husband was a multi-sport athlete who eventually followed the Grateful Dead around and lived in his van for a year. Okay, maybe we avoided social plans if a Blackhawks game was on TV. Anyway, we have Ricky to thank for two years of hockey life.

At spring break, searching for something to keep him busy, I found a 3-day hockey camp in Denver. The place was known for its Russians. Their décor was unapologetically Cold War, two very cold ice rinks with a few solitary benches at ice-level. From the lobby, the spectators were led upstairs where foldable metal chairs used for poker games were available. Some chairs were already set up and lined alongside the glass where one could look down at the ice rinks on either side of the room. Upstairs, the industrial carpet on the floor was stained with dark spots and small tattered holes, as if a squirrel or a raccoon had been trapped there overnight. The area was a wide-open invitation for mayhem for the younger siblings of hockey players who had been dragged along. They had an unofficial dedicated space to run around without supervision. There was an old dilapidated "bar" area that at one time could have been a place to serve refreshments, but was never developed, so it became the cursed jungle gym for kids to climb on while playing hide and seek. The place smelled like the color gray and felt like the absence of hope.

For the spectators, you had to endure the occasional cries of a kid miscalculating their landing from a jump off the bar. You watched the game in virtual silence, since the glass was a barrier to any sounds of the game below. The wisdom of its design was that the glass was there to prevent you, as a parent, from interfering with training or games. Watching the players in a shootout gave one a sense of being perched up like Plutarch Heavensbee from Hunger Games in his central observation tower.

My son said he wanted to go because a famous Russian hockey player was leading the camp. This guy was 9 feet tall, his head the size of a Grizzly Bear noggin. He did not smile and barely spoke more than a few words at a time. This coach had an Olympic Gold medal from playing on the Russian Unified Team (former Soviet Union) and also played in the NHL. I had a bunch of errands to run, so I dropped my son off in the lobby where only a handful of other kids had signed up for the 3-day camp. In Colorado, most of the people I knew were squeezing out the last dollar from their season's ski pass, feverishly driving back and forth to get their money's worth. Or they were headed out to someplace warm for spring break. That year, we had decided to stick around and avoid the added expense of a vacation or crowded slopes from tourists on their spring break. I was in no mood to get taken out at the knees by an out-of-control-blue-jean and sunglass-wearin' Texan in a Dallas Cowboys jacket. Add in high-altitude drinkin' and a few first-time pot smokers, and you got yourself a real rodeo.

Navigation Tip: Hockey camps, out-of-state games and tournaments rarely count as a vacation destination. These are your family vacations going forward. How do you feel about Fargo, North Dakota? Chicago in January? Blaine, MN in February? Occasionally there's a Vegas Trip, but those are dangerous and there's a good chance you'll be following a 12-step program at some point because of it.

Each day I picked him up from the camp, he would immediately go home, eat something, and practice his shots from the street at the end of the driveway. Again, I thought it was great he was so active. I was always congratulating myself for keeping the kids away from phones and video games (even though I had mastered PacMan and Space Invaders in 8th grade).

By the third day, I was running a little late for pickup and needed to go inside to find him. As I entered the lobby of the rink, there sat my son, next to the coach on the dilapidated bench. They were both waiting for me, my son looked like he wanted to cry so I didn't know what to expect when I approached them. I introduced myself to the coach and in his thick Russian accent he said, "this boy...should not play...AA hockey...too smart." He then pointed to a large poster on the wall that had a bunch of hockey players plastered across with some dates for spring hockey tryouts. He looked at me, then pointed again to the poster and said, "Pee Wee year is the most important year. Fundamentals. This boy, too smart for AA hockey...play AAA," and walked away on his skates without any response from me.

I stood there, not sure if I had peed in my pants a little, but fairly certain he had grown another foot and his head was somehow bigger. I looked at my son, who may have also peed in his pants a little. He had tears in his eyes, gulped and said, "Mom...can I try out?"

2

THE HOOK AND REEL

At the "advanced" age of 12 our son embarked on the path toward AAA hockey. This meant that our 4-minute commute time to the YMCA had just jumped to 55 minutes of highway driving past Denver. We had to figure out which was more important: missing a soccer game or a hockey tryout. Wanna take a wild guess on what he chose? Ding ding ding, the hockey tryout.

At age 12, decisions need to be made. Although multi-sport athletes apparently still exist, factor in (1) the number of children in the family; (2) the number of parents available to drive; (3) cost; (4) distance; and (5) how important family dinners are to your family. The fantasy of the small-town athlete making it to a Division 1 (D1) college is a myth unless you live in Minnesota, certain parts of the east coast or you're part of the Detroit hockey mafia. Even then, by the time a boy is 12, he better start thinking about what sport he loves the most and just choose. Some real Sophie's Choice shit.

We told the soccer coach that it appeared this would be our son's final season and could see the disappointment in his eyes. Soccer was also getting more competitive and kids were starting to leave their local programs for the travel programs. The cream was rising to the top, so those players considered more "elite" were also needing to choose. Gone were the days of really good games made up of competitive teams that played close to their homes. Everyone scattered in hopes of finding their promised land, whether that be playing on a team where all the kids were just as good as the next, or putting them in the sightlines of college scouts. Or maybe it just means you have the cash to make it happen.

Needless to say, hockey was calling our son loud and clear, so he finished out the soccer season without any fanfare, and we started writing bigger checks. We were scoobing the dooby and getting hooked from taking bigger hits from the proverbial hockey pipe. There are books[1] written about the American trend toward paying an inordinate amount of money for youth sports. You should read them.

AAA, or "checkbook hockey" as some say, is a very interesting business model. It starts with a moment of *recognition* much like a waitress in a bar gets discovered by a Hollywood agent passing through. Marry the notion of recognition with passion and desire of the player, and you've got yourself a deal.

The spring hockey tryout is a bit of a misnomer at the age of 12. It's a way for the coaches to sort out who is potentially going to make their team for the next season under the guise of fun and development. The kids are from all over the board, some are definitely going to play as you can tell by their confidence and helmet thumps by the coach. The next round of kids, the try-hards, will give all they have on the ice but not quite the skill level that the coaches will need. They will make the team in the fall if the roster is short. The final group of kids seem to enjoy hockey but just don't have the athleticism or desire to play at a competitive level. Maybe they like baseball but Dad really wants them to play hockey. Look for Daddy-o in the stands with a look of disappointment or mannerisms like crossing arms, giving hand signals then throwing them up in the air as he turns away.....exasperated.

As the tryouts wrapped up, the spring hockey roster reflected that the organization did not cut anyone. Everyone makes it at the age of 12 in Colorado, especially if there is enough space on the list. They need the money. If there are other spring hockey organizations that are better or have a less expensive model, the distribution of "talent" gets spread thinner therefore affording a more generous entrance into the program. Luckily, we were completely naïve at the time and just thought it was exciting to play for a different "level" of hockey with a coach that had some street cred like the NHL and the Olympics.

Navigation Tip: Find the good coaches who teach fundamentals. Vince Lombardi, one of the most famous football coaches in history, was famous for starting his training camps with a statement, "Gentlemen, this is a football." He treated each player like a blank slate. In our case, the Grizzly Bear was our Vince Lombardi. Dumb luck.

Spring hockey in and of itself was uneventful but truly was an eye-opener for my son who had never seen a full sheet of ice for a practice. He was over the moon excited to attend practices 3 times a week with games on the weekend. We were going to get the 9-foot tall Russian as a coach who immediately went to work teaching the players tape-to-tape passing and made them practice fundamentals over and over again. He would have the goalie move from the net to demonstrate a shot from the blue line saying things like, "move or this will kill you." His old school Soviet-era drills included diving on the ice, getting up, passing the puck and being ready to score. It was all about repetition. Puck control. Passing. Shooting. Skating. He progressed each skill as a distinct step before introducing the players to higher level drills. The kids would have white salt streaks on their faces from the sweat and loss of electrolytes. I remember overhearing a mom expressing her concerns to another mom about the kids being worked too hard. I knew at that moment that she was a goner. Wuss.

Navigation Tip: Find a family to carpool with, it makes the commute a little more bearable and enables social downtime for the kids. There is no need to watch every practice, it's like going to school and watching your kid learn math. Waste of time and gas, save it for later when you have no choice.

At the end of the season, my husband and I reluctantly agreed to go forward despite all of the reasons not to (commute, cost, travel, time suckage). We accepted the fact that we lived in an area of the country where pond hockey was rare and kids that really wanted to play had to drive far. The fall tryouts went swimmingly, our son had no trouble making the team. Essentially, everyone with the exception of just a few kids from the spring team all made it (mom who complained about drills and whose kid was a grocery stick, we never saw again).

Non-hockey people: *A grocery stick is the kid who sits on the bench dividing up the defensive and the offensive players, they don't get to play. Mostly useless. No kid wants to be that kid.*

We would soon find out that this team of "elite" players was elite for only that spring team, and our work would be cut out in the form of losses in the double digits.

3

CROSSING THE RUBICON

D eciding to play for a AAA team at the age of 12 will get you a bunch of grumpy snickering from your old friends at the YMCA:

- *"Why would you spend the money?"*
- *"He'll burn out once they start hitting in Bantam."*
- *"You shouldn't do it, you're wasting college money, or worse, your own retirement!"*
- *"You'll never get to ski...don't even bother getting a pass."*
- *"You'll never go on a decent vacation again. What about your other kids?"*
- *"Get ready to start bartending because unless you win the lottery, you will hemorrhage money."*

I was too old to make extra money by harvesting eggs from my ovaries to pay for hockey. Just kidding, but I *was* starting to wonder how we were going to afford this. The comments came from family too; questions on how much hockey would cost, and why we were allowing it, were common. All of these honest questions and snide remarks were foreshadowing. It reminded me of when I was a new mother, trying to shop for groceries while my kid was wailing. I'd mutter words like "he's teething" and some old hag would tell me to put whiskey on my baby's gums to stop the pain. Back off lady, I think I know what I'm doing! I don't need your advice. Freak.

You have to ask yourself: is it because your kid really wants it? Or because you do? This is important. Unless the kid is watching the game on his own, practicing his shot on a daily basis and looking for ways to get on the ice, it's not worth the exorbitant fees. Let them play A or AA for a while longer. Any serious athlete will tell you they were *obsessed.*

Or maybe their dad was obsessed and in order to please him, the kid was obsessed. Oh yeah, there's some intense father-son shit out there, lots of hovering over the kid like he's the next hockey Messiah. In some cases, it pays off, but the risk of resentment is there too. Plenty of examples of that across all sports.

I observed that the happiest AAA athletes had an *authentic* devotion to the sport at the ages of 11 and 12. The parents were not planning the route to a Division 1 college yet, they were just trying to be supportive. However, when signing the 4-figure check for the season, I would say *"thousand"* out loud just to make it sting my psyche. A little wave of cautious optimism would make me feel better. Old-school hockey parents would call it spoiling your child.

Navigation Tip: What are you willing (and able) to spend (time and money)? You may not be able to answer this but do a quick gut-check at the end of the season.

One day, my son came home from middle school and asked me if there was something wrong with him. I asked him, "what do you mean, are you feeling alright?" Having an Italian mother and being raised in a constant state of worry regarding health problems, I am obsessed with food and death. He didn't look hungry or sick but inevitably my thoughts went to being bullied, having an unexplained lump or a crush on a girl.

But then he responded, "When I'm sitting in school listening to the teacher, all I can think about is hockey."

I asked him what he meant, as I wasn't sure if he was developing ADHD or just had a boring teacher.

He answered, "It's just that I can't stop thinking about it, so I was wondering if I could get a better setup in the garage so if I practice more, maybe I'll get sick of it and won't think about it as much." This was a brilliant tactic to get new things, and of course being a pushover for any activity that encouraged my kids to be physically active, I laughed it all off and proceeded to research good deals for a new setup.

The hockey net we had purchased him was falling apart because he was moving it every day from inside our garage, down the slope and to the street. Hockey pucks were all over the place. Our neighbor complained that there were a few dents on his house's siding from our kid missing the net from the street. His shot was getting stronger and we needed to contain it. So, we found a shooting tarp that we could set up across the back of the garage and purchased a new hockey net. The tarp was hung from the ceiling about 1 foot in front of the garage fridge. I hated it. I could no longer park my car in the garage and felt like I was being kidnapped from behind any time I tried to put extra groceries away as the door could only open to fit a gallon of milk sideways. We found a small 5x7 plastic shooting pad online, and eventually got some synthetic ice tiles and a Passmaster so he could practice shots off the garbage cans.

Christmas and birthdays were only hockey stuff. The grandparents got into it because they liked watching him skate under the viaduct near our house. Not much outdoor ice in Colorado, we get about 2 weeks of legit pond hockey and then people start falling in, so we relied on frozen patches under the shaded viaduct. Well, maybe we had the only hockey-obsessed kid who did that. Good thing he didn't know who Pennywise was either.

My husband decided to cover the garage lightbulb with an old grill from a hockey helmet that we found and the kid went to town. Within a few days, we noticed chunks of drywall, dented storage bins and hockey pucks appearing in every single crevice or plastic bin in the garage. Thwoop...Thwoop....Ding....Thwoop...click click click... Thwoop. Garage up, garage down, he started shooting pucks after school and right before bed. Same neighbor asked if he could stop his activities a little earlier since his kids went to bed around 8 pm. Sure, we said as we giggled about the errant pucks on his roof.

I asked, "How many shots are you aiming for in a day?"

He replied, "I wanna try for 500 shots a night - this guy on YouTube said that's how you get better."

So, if your kid is taking it upon themselves to improve and suggesting ways to make it happen, then AAA hockey is a great idea. If it translates to watching hockey games on TV or how-to videos on YouTube, you may thank your lucky stars that these items are free and take advantage of the fact that this is the only thing that is free from here on out. Unless you are lucky and have people in your life who give great hockey advice.

The first season of AAA was a bit of a disappointment. There was a coaching change after we signed our first check. BAMBOOZLED right out of the gate, but what are you gonna do? The main guy that encouraged us to try out, The Russian skills coach (a. k. a. Grizzly Bear), was going to devote his energy to coaching the 15-year olds, who just *happened* to have 2 kids from Russia who were amazing hockey players. They had a decent shot of making the USA Hockey Nationals (they lost in the final game, by the way) so his traveling days would be limited to their schedule. We would still have him as our day-to-day practice coach as this guy was enslaved to being on the ice 6-8 hours a day. They told us they would find a different coach for our team when we traveled and would notify us once they had made the selection. We stayed out of politics, as we could see some of the returning parents were furious and threatening a coup. The owner of the rink was a stodgy, grumpy man who rarely spoke to parents. We contained any feigned feelings of outrage as we were just looking forward to a new season free from baggage and known offenders.

At the age of 12, my son didn't have any hangups about the path, he only knew that he wanted to be ready for Grizzly Bear drills and a different AAA coach the next season. Going into his second year of Pee Wee as a 12-year old, his only option was stick-and-pucks that summer at the YMCA. We had not yet drunk the Kool-Aid for summer hockey camps.

We printed out the schedule for the YMCA's stick-and-pucks and learned that the process of signing up for these skates was cumbersome. As a parent, you could get a spot on the ice for your kid if they signed their name on the clipboard within 24 hours, no more. Anyone under the age of 13 needed a guardian to do it. They did not accept phone registrations and nothing was online. So we had to drive there....twice. Welcome to the 1970s.

Anyway, I sucked it up and complied because I could justify a stop to the adjacent coffee shop creating an associative learning pattern that coffee equals hockey. One day, a young coach (Mario) was giving private lessons at the YMCA and asked my son where he learned how to skate. The two struck up a conversation and Mario offered to help him get ready for the AAA season. He knew the program and liked the way my kid was handling the puck. Mario had endured a career-ending injury at his D1 college a few years before and had only been teaching learn-to-skate programs after coming to grips with the end of his NHL dream. He seemed nice, he was really funny, and the kids all liked him; so I brought my son to a few lessons.

Mario had my son pushing tires on the ice and performing creative stickhandling drills in the same private lesson - all for $20 an hour. Sure, why not? After a few lessons, I could see that this young coach saw something in him that reminded him of himself; they developed a simpatico relationship. It was like having the older brother who played hockey, he warned him of locker-room bullying, coaching favorites, importance of grades and working hard. He gave his personal copy of a book that had been on his nightstand called, "So You Want to Play in the NHL: A Guide for Young Players" by Dan Bylsma. Mario told him to never give up on the dream because the dream is possible unless someone or something interferes. He talked about confidence and that no person could give you confidence, you get confident by practicing and learning how to take and apply constructive criticism. He stressed being coachable. He lamented his own injury and told us to be prepared for a lot of ups and downs. But to always have fun no matter what.

In the words of Dorothy from the Wizard of Oz, "It's not where you go, it's who you meet along the way." I gave Mario an extra $10 at each lesson, justifying it as extra pay for all the life lessons. He was one of the good ones.

To my reader at this point in the book, I bestow a good luck spell on your player that they are fortunate to get one of the good ones in the early years. Unfortunately, my wizardry is not powerful enough to go beyond private lessons.

After a nice summer of stick-and-puck-life-lessons, we went to the first parent's meeting of the season for his first AAA team. Most of the parents were still grumbling about feeling bamboozled. We were just happy to have kids on the team who really wanted to play competitive hockey. They announced our coach who would be the one at all the games. Alas, a dad coach. This coach also happened to be a sports agent...for the NFL. Most of the kids were certainly impressed by his client list, but unimpressed by his coaching talents. He had a few moves and some catchy phrases he must have lifted from motivational sports posters, but that was about it. He tried.

The true development happened for our team at the practices and scrimmages. The Russian skills coach (Grizzly Bear) had their souls five times a week for 75 minutes. No drama. The Grizz would demonstrate the drill, expect the kids to replicate it, and if they didn't, he would smack the stick so hard on the ice that it sounded like gunfire. The reverb was deafening and would hang in the air as the first skater attempted the drill. Not all kids thrived in this environment, but all of them got used to it. My kid loved it.

Like the Grizz said, the Pee Wee years are the most important years for learning the fundamentals. If your kid is coachable and the focus is on the development, it doesn't matter if they rack up points or not. What really matters is if they're applying what they learn. It certainly helps if they have a good skills coach. My kid got his ass handed to him at every practice. No amount of catchy motivational quotes was going to help him. Thank God for the Russians, they don't mince words but make it fun in their own twisted way. If he said "dah" that meant the player was exceptional. If he yelled or smacked his stick on the ice, that meant the player *should* be able to perfect it and the stick was Pavlovian for "get it right next time." If he didn't say anything, it meant the kid was not worth his breath. It was *that* simple and corrective. No drama. Shockingly fun.

At this point in my life, I was already weathered from raising four kids in my house. I suppose if my hockey player was used to being mollycoddled, he wouldn't have made it very far. I was capable of separating my emotions from what was happening to my child on the ice. He chose this sport, not me. He enjoyed the rigorous practices on the ice. He wanted the terse corrections and repetitions. He was *not* looking for a warm and fuzzy coach who encouraged him to try harder, he wanted to know what the hell it was going to take to get better. His choices were predicated on a fervent desire to excel in this sport. He absolutely loved it more than anything else in the world. If I had a theme song for this development phase, it would be "O Fortuna" from Carmina Burana which literally means "oh fate." Put this music to the video of your player getting bag skated in practice and you'll know exactly why this song is perfect.

Non-hockey people: Bag skated is a way for coaches to prove a point. A little bit motivation and a little bit of torture, kids need extra red meat in their diet that week.

One of the most popular phrases in competitive sports is that "it is a marathon, not a sprint." I would rather stab myself nine times and soak in a tub of leeches than actually ever run a marathon. However, it is a phrase that gets the parents through a cruddy season. Consider getting it as a tattoo, as it will be a constant mantra from this day forward.

When you shell out $8K for a season fee, another grand for uniforms and equipment, and throw in an extra $8K for the travel (plane fare, hotel, car and food for either both parents or just one and the kid), you start thinking about what you could do with that money each year. The first year of AAA is all about getting you in the "club" hockey mentality, so they bring you in like any respectable drug dealer would. Remember the gateway drug? The small tokes, maybe one over the line? It starts by offering you entrance to various tournaments in Chicago, Minnesota, Detroit, Toronto, and Boston with the lure that you could end up going to the Pee Wee Quebec tournament. So, you pay your fee, already feeling pretty proud of yourself that you are giving your kid every chance to pursue their passion and their dreams. Unless you already live in Minnesota, maybe Michigan or certain parts of New England, it is improbable for your kid to go to a public high school with high-caliber hockey. There was no real way to let him fight his way up through the ranks of other hockey obsessed kids. You have to pay heaps of money for the experience and the dream. As my grandpa would say, "What a racket!"

Minnesota, albeit with its own issues, has it right. You go to school, play hockey with your friends, play pond hockey with kids that are better than you, and hope to get scouted with the other mega hockey players in that universe.

The hangup with travel clubs is the checkbook. It is not an even playing field, you have kids who probably love the sport but whose parents aren't willing or able to give up their retirement savings or for that matter, anything they would have saved for college, to the sport. Think about the book/movie "The Blind Side " here, there are probably a few Michael Oher's out there just needing a wealthy family to adopt them. You see, these fees add up to four years of college if you start playing in travel leagues at a young age. The conundrum is that you don't get "better" if you wait too long. Most of these teams (especially in Detroit) start out together when they are 10,

11, 12 years old. The best kids start to figure out how to get on the best teams with the best coaches, which is also a complete circus. Lots of politics and hockey dads with line charts, at least we dodged that shitshow. In Colorado, our hockey communities are too dispersed to create a hockey mafia, or at least that wasn't our experience.

New England high schools and prep schools have their own regional woes but high school hockey is competitive. Again, where you live and what high school you go to may not get you the best team or development. I lived in New England for three years, and definitely noticed some provincialism. Different kind of money. I'd be curious how many kids from Massachusetts could differentiate Colorado and Utah on a map, let alone hockey rinks west of Pittsburgh. Wyoming and South Dakota are not the west coast little Johnny. California is the coast. *FYI, coaches love to use little Johnny for any fictitious hockey player. Boys, this name is dated. Try Jacob, Ryan or Zach.*

But the New Englanders produce some good hockey players nonetheless.

You will also start to notice former NHL players with sons offering to be head coaches. When it really counts is at age 13 and 14 because the kids with the most talent are being identified. It's like a mini Game of Thrones, lots of little kingdoms with kings and princes.

You have kids where their parents are so blinded by the craziness of hockey that it becomes obsessive for them. Sometimes it is the father, who may have played in high school or college but got injured and never really fulfilled his fantasy, still hanging on to the dream by living through their son or daughter. Could be the mom that needs to fuel her own aggressiveness through being the world's biggest fan. In between obsessive and normal, there lies a whole cast of interesting characters.

～

Let's talk about hockey parents for a second.

The Dads (you can find them at any tournament):

Dad #1 - Livin' the dream: Played when they were young. Coach their own kid any chance they get. Sometimes mean. Can be seen pacing around before a game talking to other fathers who look exactly like them. Stands across the rink from the bench so they can make eye contact with their kid while he's on the ice. Secret hand signals for their kid. Can be found in the stands up top where they will yell loudly at their kid or the team, because clearly it is their yelling that will help the team win.

Dad #2 - No talking: Pleasant, chit-chats a little bit at the beginning of the game, then disappears. Often seen on ice-level, standing alone. Usually silent and a little stressed, keeps to himself.

Dad #3 - Beer-drinking social guy: Usually has a posse, a little gang of sorts. Definitely one of the frat guys of the team fathers, always ready to tailgate before, during, and after a tournament. You have to be invited in, but there is usually a core group. They drink their way through a lot together, plenty of private jokes and familiar insults between them. Their kids are usually the "better" of the players because there is a confidence level that goes along with their ability to have fun while watching the sport. This group can be intimidating to any dad who's not a big drinker or golfer or wannabe sports commentator. Not always there for the hockey. Hilarious crew but definitely a clique.

Dad #4 - Video guy: Always videos his kid. May even have a pretty expensive setup, like he owns a media company. Keeps himself busy moving the camera, which is always on his kid. Never leaves his spot.

Dad #5 - Loyal husband guy: Sits with his wife and/or parents every time. Not really sure if he *wants* to be sitting with wife, but knows better than to think he has a choice.

Dad #6 - Top bleacher guy, center ice: Doesn't care who's around him, doesn't mind people but really wants the best view of the ice, like a virtual big screen TV.

Dad #7 - Penalty box guy: Volunteers so he can telepathically control his kid's movements and help coach kids in the box and (God help us) correct the refs in case they get a goal or assist wrong. That, and gets the best seat in the house. This guy is also the guy who can work the clock. Pay him in beer.

Dad #8 - Occasional dad guy: Played another sport, or isn't really into it. Probably the divorced guy who is reluctantly paying child support and hockey expenses.

And, yes....The Moms:

Mom #1 - Cheerleader: Often has a jersey with the kid's name/number on it. Cheers really loud throughout, loves to see the team play together. Has a giant blanket and Mary Poppins bag filled with food, Bandaids, hand sanitizer and warm clothing.

Mom #2 - Cougar mom: Wears high heels, lots of makeup, and something revealing even though it's frickin' cold in the rink. Could cut the ice if she fell chest-first onto it. Looking for some kind of attention from the coaches or other dads, or maybe seeking a new hookup this season.

Mom #3 - Talker mom: Does not stop talking during a game, any topic is fair game. Avoid at all costs, you will not know what is going on and leave with a headache. May have a cowbell if she has a sore throat.

Mom #4 - Swearing mom: This mom usually f-bombs her way through the game, especially if she feels her kid is not getting enough ice time or being targeted and marked by the opponent. Does not hold back in yelling at the refs or opposing players. May take on another parent on the other side too. Doesn't give a shit what people think of her.

Mom #5 - Sweet mom: Doesn't know anything about the sport, just looking for kinship and wants to see her kid do well. This mom will not say anything bad about any kid, coach or parent. Rare find. If hot cocoa and fuzzy socks were a person, this is her. Has a sign in her kitchen that says "Family." May miss a game for church.

<u>Mom #6 - Busy mom with younger kids:</u> Usually just chasing younger siblings, getting up to get food, handing iPads or phones to siblings, trying to keep them busy for the umpteenth time because there is no place that kid would rather be than cold bleachers *not* watching their brother play hockey.

<u>Mom #7 - Goalie mom:</u> A wreck when her kid is playing. Can only speak when the puck is on the other side of the ice, notices everything about her player and has her own superstitions and rituals. Much more fun when her player is not playing, as the stress emanating from her area has its own universal aura. Sometimes moves to the end her goalie is on; has implicit superstitions that you must respect. Never tell her "He's having a great game, looks like he'll get a shut-out." It was times like these that I thank God I had a forward.

<u>Mom #8 - Scoresheet mom:</u> Most are fine, they get it right. But may have to be a little skeptical of a few. There are stories of volunteers who were masters at manipulating the scoresheet for the benefit of their player. They now work for crypto startups.

These are just a few samples of typical characters from US youth hockey. Plenty more archetypes; social media memes are capturing their essence fairly well if you need validation of your own tendencies. Perhaps some day there will be a Myers-Briggs test or new Zodiac sign that will help us understand this phenomenon of "typical" hockey parents. The attributes are comically similar across the country.

In any case, the second Pee Wee year should still be fun for the parents. There are glimpses of greatness in almost every player on the ice, but the next hockey proteges are still in contention. It is true that the next Sidney Crosby is perhaps already showing up at tournaments, but it is highly unlikely your kid has really gone through all of those critical small area games[1] to get to that level. What I know is that our team sucked, and we found ourselves losing by mercy rules and double digits. It is never a good sign when your coach just resorts to words like "believe you can win" when the score is 18-0. That kumbaya shit works for Ted Lasso and that's about it.

Our first go-around with AAA was comical. There was one time our coach (the one who was an agent for football players) brought a famous player from the Denver Broncos to help motivate the bench. Half of the kids were so star-struck they forgot they were playing hockey. A few kids were annoyed because they didn't care about football at that moment, they just wanted to save face and get back on the ice.

It was clear that our season was not going to get much better despite the awesome fundamentals the players were being taught by The Grizz. It was also clear that our program did not qualify for the Quebec Pee Wee tournament which, from what I understand, is amazing and fun and the equivalent of a year of boarding school. I wish we could have gone, because this would have filled an entire chapter for this book. According to fellow parents, you unlock another level of stories once you cross the border into Canada. If I had liked video games, which, remember, *I DON'T,* it would be akin to an "experience point" that changes your life. If a kid works hard, listens to the coach and minimizes the goofing around, they'll get better despite the wins and losses. My son seemed calm about all of the team's losses; he told me it didn't matter if they won that year, he just wanted to get better. From the mouth of babes.

4

TIME TO GET SERIOUS

In the western states, we have a bunch of rinks and hockey programs, but for some reason we can't seem to get a consolidated team with heavy competition for tryouts. The "talent" is spread all around the state and eventually people decide how far they want to drive. In some cases, people send their kids to billet. This is when you send your player to live with a family in another state who is willing to adopt them for the hockey season. Talk about trust.

Our son decided it was best to drive as far as possible within the state rather than the AAA team that was located about 15 minutes from our house. In his defense, the organization that was 50 miles away had the reputation for developing some noticeable talent. Kids are easily impressed when they find a website with a splash page advertising former players who have made it to the NHL. It leaves an impression that if you play here, you'll get what you need to make it. In his age group, the kids had some notoriety as being the fastest and most skilled in the state, already they were making names for themselves. Thus, if your kid wanted to try out for a team where they could play with kids who were not only obsessed with hockey but also highly skilled, you had to be willing to make the longer drive.

Time for spring hockey and trying out for a new team. We'd been through this once before, but we knew this time it would be different. More competitive.

By the age of 13, body checking is allowed in USA hockey. This age classification is called Bantam and for many kids, learning how to check (and how to take a hit) meant a specialty camp. Three days was enough to weed out the faint of heart (this could mean the parents just as much as the kids). Some kids left limping and talking about summer baseball. Spring hockey also meant springing for the better breezers that had thicker pads. Ouch, those continuous hip checks practices left some nice bruises.

We registered for the spring hockey tryout and received some information about the next 8 weeks of hockey life. Only a select number of kids would make either Team "A" or "B," with plans to attend the tournament in Minnesota in May. Needless to say, my son was shitting bricks because he had never played with or against any of these kids before. Since the rink was a minimum of 60 minutes of driving, we gave ourselves an extra 30 minutes. We drove west, staring directly into the sun in a car without adequate air conditioning, so my son was feeling nervous and extremely nauseated in preparation for his tryout. When we arrived, I deposited him at the front table, checked him in and decided to run out to Starbucks for an icy drink and some Tylenol for my own headache. He left his phone in the car, per my request. I wished him good luck and off he went!

When I returned, all the parents were seated in the stands, anxiously awaiting their future NHL prospect's tryout. I squeezed in by one of the dads from our old team and we sat watching 50 kids all trying to prove themselves to the future coaches of the U13 spring team.

Now, there are plenty of reasons to *not* watch tryouts. This is up to your kid. My kid was fine with it, but some players get nervous because their parents are in the stands. This was a non-issue for us. However, that day I noticed my son looked really "off" in the way he was handling the puck. He was getting to all the right places and skated correctly, but seemed to have some hex on his stickhandling, as if he was being controlled by a wicked marionettist.

He was one of 4 players with a white helmet, so I could spot him as he got on and off the ice. The old team was amazing, as they easily out-skated and out-scored anyone else at the tryout. They clearly were the chosen ones, fist-pumping and having loads of fun after coming off of their Pee Wee season with a decent record and tons of confidence. Everyone else on the ice was crazed, very desperate with little glimpses of knowing how to play hockey with the chosen ones. There was still another day of a hockey tryout, so I collected my son and asked him how the kids treated him on the bench and in the locker room. He looked upset. Apparently, he had forgotten his gloves at home. He couldn't find me so he went to the hockey shop and asked for help, not knowing what else to do. The guy helped him find another adult man who had some gloves he said he could borrow, XL men's gloves. My son had no choice, so hence his bizarre modern dance stickhandling scenario. He said, "Mom, it was like taking bubble wrap and putting it around your hands and trying to blow dry your hair, or do your makeup, that's what it was like. It sucked."

Of course, I could have sympathized, but my reaction (therefore making me a true hockey parent) was to tell him that the first rule of hockey is to make sure you have everything you need in your bag. It was not my responsibility to remember, it was his. Because of this life lesson, he would never do it again. And he didn't (except that time he forgot his gym shoes for dryland at a 4-day tournament, did the drills in dress shoes! Bwahhhaaa!). I patted him on the back and told him to just focus on day two, things would work out. Then I felt bad. Maybe I should have helped him out, but I had a lifetime of Catholic guilt and this did NOT amount to eating meat on a Friday during Lent.

Navigation Tip: It isn't your responsibility to make sure everything is in your kid's hockey bag. It's their responsibility to get their shit together.

The next day, he triple-checked his bag and fortunately managed to return the 40-year old man's gloves. Good hockey karma.

As he skated out on the ice, I could see he had to prove himself. Watching his body language, he seemed confident and ready. On his first shift, he scored a goal. Second shift, assisted the goal. Third shift, seeing the ice and creating beautiful plays until it was clear that he had redeemed himself (to himself). I kept hearing the veteran dads say "Who is that kid in the white helmet?" as he easily started meshing with the kids on the current team.

Needless to say, he made the spring team. They had to cut some of the players due to keeping the size of practices to normal numbers, so 38 kids were invited back.

For the next 3 weeks, I watched a few of his practices, noticing that my son would always hang back to avoid getting in the way of the current team. He must not have felt worthy, but when he actually played, he showed up for himself. I noticed that he would gravitate to his old teammate and only hang out with him. I told him he needed to start owning his skills and be okay with being the first kid out there, the first one to kneel when the coach was explaining a drill, the kid who helped gather the pucks or stay on the ice to fix the net for the Zamboni, etc. These are all the character traits and habits a coach is looking for. Well, he barely did any of that and still resorted to hanging back as much as possible. Toward the end of the practices, he started to improve. I noticed he was more jovial with the other kids and appeared to be a bit more earnest with his line up in the drills and helping out. Slow and steady won the race in his book.

One day, I received a call from the head coach for the spring team, he was a phenomenal ex-NHL player named Pavel. He asked if my son could play in an unofficial scrimmage. He was to show up at 7 am, have a white jersey and be ready to play. Lo and behold, there were all the former team members from the U12 team plus my son and one other defenseman. He did fine, held his own and there was no feedback or conversation, just awkward eye contact with people who didn't know me and whom I didn't know. I found out the next weekend that another kid was asked to scrimmage alongside the team, so I assumed he was not the "it" guy after all, since there was obviously only one spot open for a forward on the team. Felt like breadcrumbing, very non-committal.

On to the spring tournament, there was one more step to the process. A scrimmage would determine who made the "A" and "B" teams for the Minnesota trip. The game looked discombobulated, kids desperately trying to prove themselves in front of the coaches. More coaches were involved this time, all perched up high in a viewing area watching each player and writing things down. At one point, my son in the white helmet was asked to switch his jersey and move to the other bench, away from his former line mate. This part was nerve-racking because they were doing so well but looking back it was all in an effort to get him to play with his future teammates. He meshed well, adjusting to his new line and seemingly earning a spot.

When the list came out, he had made the "A" team alongside all of the past season's AAA team. Only one other kid, a defenseman, had squeezed out a former member of the team (apparently it was known that he was getting voted off the island).

Unfortunately, his wing man and former teammate made the "B" team. That kid's dad was livid and proceeded to criticize the process, the politics, the overarching bias of the coaches who were clearly buddy-buddy with the dads. I learned, from the past season, to just shut up and try to help by nodding and sighing along every scathing comment. Just like the owner of a funeral home, offer sympathies, hold hands in front of you and maintain a neutral frown.

Navigation Tip: Don't say shit. The hole in the middle of your face....zip it.

I have learned to practice this awkward social situation from years of managing an IT team in Chicago. Oftentimes, high profile projects run by powerful executives meant that I had to take the blame for anything that went wrong because of underfunded technology which my team was responsible for maintaining. I was middle-management for a company that supported the Board of Trade and other financiers in downtown Chicago. My team affectionately referred to me as a dude with boobs. Or a chick with nuts? I don't remember. I guess it was a compliment in the late 90s.

The intensity of the environment was an abusive relationship insofar as our team was treated like a punching bag. If a trade went bad, it could easily be blamed on faulty IT architecture. I had a guy throw his laptop across the room when I told him he was responsible for keeping his computer charged. Had to do that with a straight face, no emotion. My role was to motivate and keep my team from quitting; there were many long hours after close of business when I would set up meetings with my "understanding" tone and facial expressions to make amends. Acting dull while you seem to care....a little. This skill I had mastered over 10 years in Corporate America prison came in handy for hockey.

Navigation Tip Reiterated: Don't say anything to fuel the fire of another hockey parent, it only makes the situation worse for them, and it will come back to you. Just offer support; don't lean in with anything extra. Your role is Innocent Bystander, and boy, it gets really hard as the years go on. Wait for the day a player you love gets cut.

After the dust settled, it was off to Minnesota. I traveled with my son and we dropped our stuff off at the team hotel. We decided to go to a nearby restaurant and saw three men sitting at a table who waved us over. I had no idea who they were, but my son said they were on the "A" team. Ugh, I had to socialize with the dads. Time to put my Corporate America Game face on again...

Fortunately, they were all very nice, and asked us all the basics: where were we from, did he like the team, how many kids did we have, what school, blah blah blah. The boys all sat at the table and were playing some weird game on their phone; my son looked like he wanted to evaporate into thin air. He had not been truly accepted into the wolf pack yet. He needed to earn his spot amongst the cubs.

There were four games. I would politely acknowledge the dads I had met but just sat by myself on the bleachers. I guess there *was* always one "keep-to-herself" mom at every game, another invisible archetype (or goalie mom, sometimes they just need more space). One of the dads was very sweet, always coming over for a few seconds between periods to tell me how well my son was playing. To me, my son looked nervous and unsure of himself, but was managing to pass the puck and make a few assists. I remember just sitting straight up, holding my breath the entire weekend.

It wasn't until the final tournament game that I realized he was doing all the right things to earn his spot. He had put some points up and according to the dads, the kid with the white helmet was *killin' it*. They were down 2-0 to a team out of Chicago, and he had a one-timer in the second period that somehow rallied the team. In another minute, a kid from his team scored another goal, tying up the game. In the third period my son worked really well with his makeshift line and they scored two more goals, winning the championship 4-2. The boys, per hockey custom, threw off their gloves and sticks and started huddling around and celebrating. My son was still insecure, skating hesitantly up to the group. A couple of the boys pulled him into the melee but I could tell he still was not feeling like he was part of the team. This was still a trial for him. If it were me, I'd be in the center relishing that I'd been a part of the momentum for the win in the championship game, but my guy was still walking with his tail between his legs. Weird.

The coaches said nothing to me, and I said nothing to them: I was not part of the parent group who was always in a posse hanging out with each other, videotaping shifts, beer drinking and gambling on games with the coaches. Apparently, this was a dad's weekend, so I was flying solo all the way through with the white helmet kid. Chicago all over again.

For example, back in my Corporate days, co-workers and I would head out after work for drinks to decompress after a stressful week. A few guys would branch off to go home to their families, a few more would head to strip clubs. Not being a strip club aficionado, I got used to being excluded. Water off a duck's back. Rookies should know their place, and I knew mine.

We had a couple of weeks before the tryouts for the U13 AAA team. The coaches were both former NHL players, one of which was widely acclaimed. For lack of a better term, I called him Hockey Jesus, but for this story, his name was Pavel. He was trying out life as a youth hockey coach and wanted to coach his kids. The other coach (Lukas) had also retired recently, not as much hockey fame but I didn't feel too sorry for him or his 20 million dollar salary. My son was looking forward to good coaching and kids who played the game the way he wanted to: competitively. He told me he would make their team, using some self-talk-Jedi-mind-trick for confidence.

Not me. This GenX Mom nails down a Plan A and a Plan B. I had seen too many unfenced goat rodeos growing up in the '80s (classic latchkey kid). I told my son he should still try out for the AAA team that had a beautiful practice facility 10 minutes from our house. He said, "Ok I'll do that, but I *am* going to make the other team." This coming from the kid who could barely make eye contact with the coaches and stayed quiet on the bench most days, just doing his job when he was on the ice to earn his keep.

Because I loved writing checks to this damn sport, I paid the $150 fee to *both* teams and off he went. He was quite the force out there for the first weekend of Plan B tryouts. Many of the kids that had been on the "B" team from the faraway spring program were at this team's fall tryout. They knew the other team was, for the most part, pre-selected. The coach, a young guy who had seen my son play at a few stick-and-pucks, called me and said he definitely had a spot on the team. I hesitated, then spilled the beans. I said he really wanted to make the "better" AAA team (Plan A) and was going to risk it. He recommended I call the coach (pre-tryout) and ask! *What??* It felt like insider trading and my neurotic guilt gave me an instant migraine. I talked about it with my husband. He brushed off any semblance of criminality like dandruff and told my son that's what we needed to do. The "B" team was asking for a check and contract *before* the "A" team had their tryouts, so in essence, you risk not playing any hockey that season if your gamble doesn't pay off.

So that evening, I decided to lock myself in my office and call the Plan A coach (Pavel). He answered on the 3rd ring. Gulp. I said "Hello" and told him that my son had tried out for the other AAA team who was asking for money and a signed contract. My next statement was even more direct: I needed to know right then and there if he should accept or decline the offer to be on the other team. As an outsider to this team, I knew this was unorthodox, but I wanted to hedge the bet. A puck in the hand is worth two in the...never mind.

The coach plainly told me, "Yes, he will be on the team." And we hung up.

I stood there, not sure if I was happy or not, feeling a little dirty, a little relieved, a little proud. So I called the first coach (Plan B-guy) back and politely declined and he agreed with me that it was the right decision for my son. I wasn't Martha Stewart selling off thousands of shares right before the stock plummeted, it was just a phone call. Right?!?!

Navigation Tip: Trust your gut. You need to make decisions that make or break the next step, even if unorthodox.

My son tried out for this highly competitive AAA team as if he was *fighting* for his spot. Good for him, not trusting adult conversations. Perched high above in the bar area were three coaches and about five other coach-looking dudes. This was quite the operation, so nerve-racking and daunting. All the parents were there, nothing was stopping the spectacle of this important year. The scrimmage was the tryout. The "A" team was mixed in with many of the "B" team plus a bunch of kids that showed up from out of state and who-knows-where to try out for the heck of it. The true "A" team was confident, fast, athletic and skilled. There were only 2 spots, one forward and one defensemen. There was also a spot for a mystery goalie who was already chosen from another team. This was sad to me since I counted at least 6 goalies trying out, but this decision was meant to be kept quiet so as not to alienate that team, who still had a few games with him. Funny, for an outsider, even *I* knew that the mystery goalie had been given a spot without even showing up for the tryout.

Navigation Tip: Buy the Apple Watch, it'll remind you to breathe, or at least alert the fire department that you're in cardiac arrest. And don't be surprised if the team is already picked in advance; have alternate plans or a good consolation speech prepared.

Anyway, tryouts went well for my son. He meshed nicely with the kids, but there were a few others who appeared to hold space as a possibility. Not knowing who to trust, we just waited for the list to come out. After the first tryout, some of the kids were cut and another day of scrimmage was set for the next day. My son's name was on the list to play again, so round one equaled a small exhale. The next day, the scrimmage was evenly split with a few kids who were all earnestly vying for the forward spot. My son told me he was pretty sure he was better but not 100% sure he would get it, despite our dirty little secret. But behold, the list came out and he'd made the team. The other new defensemen and my son had such a look of relief on their faces. There was no doubt that this was a good day in hockey.

After a little revelry, I noticed the families walking out with the boys who had been cut. Their sweaty heads hung low, bodies slumped over, holding their heavy hockey bags and avoiding eye contact with anyone around them. The mom or dad holding the door open, keys in hand and trying to be friendly to people attempting to console their player as if someone had died or lost the family pet. Some men simply did a quick nod, acknowledgement to the ritual of trying out, getting cut and moving on to another club or Rec league. The hardest ones are the people who were part of the team the year before, as those families feel like they're being divorced. Some very sad goodbyes that day in the lobby.

For my family, we were overjoyed and relieved. We had endured 10 weeks of sheer stress, from the first day of encouraging my son to try out for the spring team, to the last day of striving to make the official team for the season. There were no guarantees, but rather a sincere fear in the back of our minds that he would need his Plan B because anything can happen in hockey. We knew there was only one forward spot because somebody was definitely getting cut. We crossed our fingers until we saw his name on the list, feeling a little sadness for the kid who was going home. In that moment, I realized that the only thing to do was to rifle through my purse and look incredibly busy while I waited for my son so we could join his new team for the first team meeting.

If your kid gets cut, just remember at this age it's not the end of the world. The kid that was cut at U13 tried out again at U15 and made the team. He just worked hard and kept practicing. Getting cut, getting rejected, feeling like you are not good enough is all part of growing up. I could be a hockey coach and say, "Some kids just don't have it," or "just keep working at it," but sometimes a kid just needs to experience rejection once to decide if the sport is worth it to them.

If they are motivated to keep going, they will find a way.

Note: Some inspirational movies include: Rudy, Soul Surfer, The Rookie, Invincible, In Search of Greatness, and Seabiscuit.

5

THE OFF-SEASON MONEY PIT

Time to refinance the house.

By the age of 13, it is increasingly difficult to have another sport in the mix. Hockey takes over as a year-long commitment, regardless of what USA Hockey or any other organization tries to tell you. It is an overgrown juniper plant, and pruning it is tedious mental work.

I'm not saying this is the best thing for your athlete. To the contrary, picking up lacrosse, tennis, golf or anything other than hockey to give their developing bodies a break is the best thing for them physically and mentally to avoid burnout. What I am saying is that the *chosen* sport is prioritized and the kid knows it. It is your job to nurture and help scout the routes, not push or spend a fortune for the alleged *best* skills camp. As a sports sherpa, you help them see that other activities are good for them to make the steep climb ahead even if you have no idea what route you are all going to end up taking.

Navigation Tip: Plan your summer by March.

~

For example, a couple of kids on the U13 team played lacrosse. They were quite talented and dominated on the field based on their competitive nature and athleticism. Put simply, they had incredible hand-eye coordination and, coming off of a hockey season, they were little gladiators already. I remember seeing them at a team-building event that involved swimming at a lake, they had six-pack abs and skinny arms. The Russian and Eastern European descendants already had tree trunks for legs as one of the advantages of being a purebred. At any given time, they may have been able to survive a blizzard or kill a bear. I digress, as I couldn't help but notice the rest of the American muts were still catching up physically and would totally lose a fight with a bear, but perhaps win a wrestling match with a fat raccoon.

Advantages of playing another sport in the summer before age 13 is that the kids play for fun, get a chance to move differently to avoid overuse injury, and are coachable. Parents often have a private conversation with the "other" coach, explaining that they may need to miss a few practices or games because of conflicts with hockey. It's understood that these kids are now called hockey players. No longer Timmy who plays hockey, lacrosse or baseball but Timmy the hockey player who plays lacrosse and baseball too. Their identity starts to cement itself as the off days are filled with skating lessons, stickhandling clinics, goalie camps or sports conditioning. This is especially true of parents that knew this about their kid all along, or perhaps their dad or brothers played hockey. It was amateur hour for us, we knew nothing.

Aside from physical activity, there are also video-game-like sports training programs. Some kids gravitate to it during their downtime, as the programs focus on cognitive performance and decision making under pressure. Bar games like foosball and shooting pool can help their social outlets later in life, perhaps a little sting pong to make it extra silly. There is always something out there that claims to help with spatial awareness, just be wary of anything involving special sunglasses or Virtual Reality. The world does not need a hockey version of the Manchurian Candidate. Plus if someone hits you in the back of the head with these special glasses on, you'll go cross-eyed. Ok, I'm making all that up but... *your eyes*!

My observation is that competitive athletes are always working on their skills because they instinctively have a growth mindset. They don't wish for it, they work for it. They don't ask themselves why they can't, they ask themselves *"how can I learn to get better?"* It is your job, as a parent, to start scouting the options for training without overwhelming the summer schedule. Remember: they still watch Star Wars movies and have lego sets; they are not collegiate athletes yet. Let's also not forget any other children you are raising in the household who don't play hockey (sorry peeps, if you have more than one hockey player in the family, you're hosed. Hopefully that extra kid isn't a goalie!).

Here's the rub.

Once you have a USA Hockey number, your email is in the universe of every camp, coach and clinic that want your money. They all sound incredible, as if Auston Matthews and Connor McDavid attributed their success to the particular coach running it. There are online coaches, mini clinics and former NHL and college coaches mixed in with average Joes who need some extra cash. There are sleep-away camps at boarding schools and for those, everything starts at $1K. You find yourself searching the internet for any sort of review of coaches and clinics and all you have is word-of-mouth marketing to really rely on.

There are so many hockey podcasts, books and hockey articles that explain what is right for your kid. It's too noisy. I would listen to a podcast and, about 3 minutes in, say, "You don't know my kid, my family, my finances, but thanks!" I did not have the time to listen to the host banter before they'd finally get to something substantive. With a mental backdrop of a constant list of tasks, I liked to unwind a bit and listen to a fiction book or health information on what supplements to take to prevent early menopause. Maybe some parents had more downtime than I did.

A word to the wise....Podcasters, cut to the chase. A little less banter please. We don't got all day!

For me, I felt very alone in this arena. I did not have any true friends yet within the team, and it seemed like everyone else had a plan but us. I could have been paranoid, but it also seemed like there was a waft of competitiveness in the secrecy around plans. When asked, parents were nonchalant, like the kid was just going to float on a raft on a lake all summer, but in reality they were already scheduled for a week in Canada at a stickhandling clinic and a week in Minnesota at an "elite" tournament your kid wasn't invited to.

I did not like this part. It made me shut down a bit and become resentful of the system. Sports are ravaging family finances, capitalism at its finest. When you're in the thick of it, you do whatever you can to keep your own kid competitive and hope you are lucky enough to find a way to help him develop *while having fun.*

If you are looking to start a valuable hockey business, create a YELP or parent-approved list for hockey camps in your region. Think about it, all other industries have this - restaurants, doctors, hotels and universities. Why not hockey? It would have helped....a lot. We have MyHockeyRankings, which was started by parents in order to sort out and competitively rank the youth hockey teams nationally. It eventually evolved into some mathematical manifest that is based on strength of schedule and other factors that people just accept as nerd-math and boom! USA Hockey uses it for who plays in the USA Nationals and anyone can see which teams have consistent programs throughout the years. So my question is, why not rate coaches and clinics?

Navigation Tip: Call around, talk to coaches and their proteges before you plunk down any money for offseason skills training. No need to lose the family farm. Did you know that trust and gambling use the same parts of the brain? You have to gut-check.

∿

In the absence of some type of catalog of reputable camps and clinics, find a kid who made the USHL[1], NAHL[2] or WHL[3] and ask what they did to "get better." There are some great coaches who never made it to the Pros as a hockey player but can train the skill of skating better than any big name. We had a coach who taught my son the biomechanics of the quick release shot. This coach had a short stint in the NHL. More impressively, he had won the Hobey Baker award decades before and was just busy being a dad and selling real estate. He wasn't advertising but loved the sport and offered private lessons at the YMCA. It was in a casual conversation at the YMCA I had learned about his willingness to coach on the side that summer. My son developed a really nice shot because of this one coach. As a spectator, it was fun to watch the coach break down the skill and see my son practicing it over and over again until he got it. Practice is important, but how they practice is even more important.

I was enlightened after I read a book on this called "The Talent Code" by Daniel Coyle. The book's subtitle is "Greatness Isn't Born. It's Grown. Here's How." Essentially, genetics is only part of the equation for amazing athletes. Most of what makes people *great* at their sport or music or art is *how* they practice. It was just one of the few books I bought over the course of supporting my developing athlete as he had to focus on his own methods to ascend the hockey mountain. After a couple of months of 5:30 am practices, it was evident that this coach was the right ingredient at the right time. He focused on a few key skills that became second nature. Building confidence one skill at a time paid off in the season. Repetition and how one practices is a huge confidence boost, but the athlete has to want to practice and perfect. Not one time did I force him to do it; he was hungry for it. All I did was send the texts to the coach to set it up. Executive Administrative Assistant sherpa.

All I am suggesting is that you work hard for your money, and if you don't have a private rink or a private coach, you can still support your future Sidney Crosby without losing your shirt. Off-season training, as they get older, becomes increasingly more important. The multi-sport athlete attempt is possible at the age of 13 and 14, but starts to wane soon after that. If you don't have pond hockey, a prep school or a ton of money, it's a lonely planet.

In the summer, we were fortunate to find a personal trainer who had developed programming just for hockey players. He was a stickler on form and was highly educated in his craft; he was usually working with collegiate and professional athletes. He looked like Mr. Clean without the hoop earring, a power lifter on his own time. Twice each summer, he would organize a run up and down the 380 steps at Red Rocks in Morrison, Colorado. He would have groups of hockey players do it 5 times in a row and someone would always puke. This guy, who was in his 30s, had trained hundreds of athletes and could beat the teenagers on the run every time. His technique, professionalism and attention to proper programming translated to sound training that spilled over into a lifetime of health and fitness. He took it seriously. He sported "smedium" tight shirts like most guys who are *just RIPPED*. And if you ever questioned the importance of pre-workout fuel or nutrition, he responded with an "in your face fatty" grin and shared what products were safe for teens.

What I appreciated was that my son was learning the value of functional fitness and the importance of off-season training at such an early age. When I was 14, I was eating Cheetos and drinking Diet Coke. Maybe I rode my bike to babysitting jobs or helped my best friend with her paper route, that was serious exercise. In any case, not everyone needs a personal trainer to do off-season training, there are plenty of online programs and facilities that have options. Just make sure that if your player is lifting weights or cross-training, they are aware of the proper ways to lift and manage nutrition.

BEWARE: The fitness industry is saturated with outdated information. Yes, eggs are still good. The Russian twist, not so good. Hard workouts are not always the smartest workouts. Again, do your research. It is highly likely YOUR high school workout is in the same class as MySpace and VHS.

How do you pay for all of this, you may ask?

Some people have high paying jobs and can afford it. Some have their own businesses or relatives that float them extra cash. In my case, I started a new business since going to work for someone else seemed impossible given my current driving and domestic duties. Not a martyr, not a hero, just a problem solver here!

In the summer of 2017, we took out a Home Equity Line of Credit and I started a business that involved flipping manufactured homes in Oklahoma. A friend of mine was the owner of a mobile home park and suggested I get into real estate for passive income. I know we needed an extra $20K/year and I didn't want this friggin' sport to take away from the rest of the family, namely my older boys that were going to college and post-secondary school.

So, I took a chunk of cash with interest accruing and went to Oklahoma. There was a mobile home park owner who was selling homes as he was converting his land to an RV park. I purchased 13 trailer homes in as-is condition and paid a specialty mover to bring them from one end of the state to the other. I considered the Shed-N-Breakfast concept from Bubbles on Trailer Park Boys, but decided I needed to flip them personally. I can write another book on how that all went, but let's just say when a city gal shows up with her own marching orders and lands in rural Oklahoma, she would do well to assume an alternate personality. I spoke differently, I looked like a Yankee, and I certainly had to check any "get it done" attitude the second I crossed the panhandle of Texas. It was at this time I was binge watching a series called "Sons of Anarchy" and boy... did I know how to channel Gemma on a good day.

My inner voice would scream at me, I learned how to bite my tongue and practice deep breathing learned from a Lamaze class that I never got to use for any of my four c-sections. Someone needs to write a Dr. Who episode about the time warp of getting handiwork done in Oklahoma. Get ready for long-winded explanations, polite people with backstories that are nothing like your hockey life, and know when someone says "Bless Your Heart," that means fuck off. There is no Jesus in that blessing, more of a middle finger without a finger. But I digress.

As I repainted walls, pulled up moldy carpet and puked in my mouth while cleaning the toilets, I quickly learned that without indoor plumbing hooked up I had to get comfortable with peeing in the empty styrofoam cup from the Love's Gas station. I also learned how to jump out of a trailer home without steps after setting off a couple of roach bombs without breaking my legs. Definitely felt like a James Bond stunt man despite my overalls and ponytail.

I lived on protein bars and leaned on the Park Manager, who was originally from Sheboygan, WI. Without her, I could not have done it. She was a tatted up, take no bullshit Wisconsin Democrat living in the middle of the Great Plains Trump-loving state. She packed heat and had my back, the best partner to deal with an area of business I knew nothing about. Her husband was an Army Veteran who I called the "Hulk" and the two of them helped me with Home Depot deliveries, contracts for the rent-to-own properties and getting electricity, water and gas hooked up with all of the utility companies.

In about 6 months, I was receiving rental income and able to make my HELOC payments. I used the extra cash for hockey sticks, camps, private lessons, hotels and plane fare. I had to make a few more trips to turnover the houses, make drywall repairs and DIY paint jobs, but I never in a million years imagined that this was going to be the way to pay for a sport. It's pretty funny looking back at the entire thing, all the things that went wrong and a few things that went right. My goal was to be done with the business and the loan in 5 years. The dichotomy of fixing up and turning over trailer homes to pay for hockey. C'mon, seriously? I just couldn't see how I was going to be able to "do what I needed to do" *and* support the overall well-being of four kids. My husband was the main breadwinner but we were both stumped on how any hockey family in this area of the country was able to do it.

And prep school? What do people do for money in New England? Does everyone have an offshore investment bond or is it grandparent cash? Mayflower money?

I also taught fitness classes, so I frequently pimped myself and offered to sub anything. Cycling, yoga, cardio, aqua-aerobics and weightlifting, I started teaching all of it in 2006 after kid #3 was born as a way to pay myself to exercise. It was fun and a great way to manage stress and utilize free daycare, otherwise I was apt to take hostages. I was the last resort sub for Zumba dance classes, definitely dug deep into my moves from 90s hip-hop and Janet Jackson videos. I would always preface each class with, "Hey I'm subbing. I am going to do my own thing up here, here's to having fun and laughing at yourself." When in doubt, I'd kick it out and lunge ala Molly Shannon as Mary Katherine Gallagher from SNL. Thank goodness the group fitness members at the gyms were a forgiving crowd, I never took myself too seriously. Typically 10 extra classes a month would pay for the new CCM stick.

As you get more familiar with the families in travel sports, you learn a lot about how people afford the exorbitant fees. One mom had a petting zoo on the weekends, another had a daycare in her basement. One dad fixed computers on the side, another mom was a hair stylist in her home. Everyone either had a side hustle or second job with at least one of the dual incomes being used for hockey. Someone always had to be available to drive to practice, pay the bills and be a mountain guide for the day.

Anyway, my long-term plan is to rely on the hockey kid to be the one to pick the nicest nursing home for us when we're old and gray and back in diapers. That's right Buddy-boy, you're going to be the one to wipe my ass someday in assisted living if my nurse quits. Or at least cry the hardest at my funeral.

Navigation Tip: Unless you have all the stupid money in the world (or a dad/brother/uncle) that already has access to premier training, your kid is going to find their own way with practice, the mental game, grit, confidence and a little bit of luck. Don't overspend; it just doesn't matter. Say it with me now: It just doesn't matter. They all end up in the beer league, even the Pros.

6

ARRESTED DEVELOPMENT

In anthropology, the term "arrested development" refers to a "sphere of development that has reached a plateau, beyond which it develops no further."[1] I propose that all male hockey players, regardless of formal education and worldly experience, have humor that is cemented by the age of 13, and there it stays. As a mother of 3 boys and perhaps not a delicate flower from growing up on the south side of Chicago, I too can say my emotional intelligence is fine but my primitive humor also stopped at the age of 13. I cannot keep a straight face, no matter how inappropriate the content.

Thirteen year old boys are literally one step above dogs, and although we want them to be respectful and socially conscious, there are no limits to their imagination when they learn how to chirp. *Chirping is trash talking. Creative insults that are the game within the game.* Hockey has its share of problems that bump up against sensitive topics like toxic masculinity, homophobic jokes, privilege and a bit o' misogyny. This is not an area I will be addressing. I'm talking about fart sounds and penis jokes. You know: the classics. I've seen grown men with NHL pedigrees snort-laugh at these jokes. Like I said: development, arrested.

The 13-year old hockey player eats mac-and-cheese, chicken

nuggets and washes it down with chocolate milk. They are only starting to learn the importance of nutrition and how it relates to their athletic performance. At travel tournaments, it's an easy sell to "make your own waffles" with fruit loops and whip cream. Prove me wrong.

Don't worry, by the age of 14 they'll be eating good protein and complex carbs. They don't care about organic or non-GMO ever, they really just need calories.

This age is fun, though they are generally exhausted from practice and often fall asleep in the car. They sometimes cry when they lose. They have crackly voices, braces, and crazy-looking long hair because they think having "flow" is really cool. *Hockey hair, usually long and untamed but can take months of nurturing to get it right. Also known as salad if the hair is thick and curly.* Back acne, face acne, athletes foot, and constant boogers are all part of the look. Adorable and scary all at the same time, they fuel their passion into practice and develop their friendships. The extra testosterone makes them skate faster, and some of them try it on for size when they are allowed to check.

They begin to develop their "role" on the team. There are the dumb-asses, the funny ones, the quiet and surly, the Christians, and the instigators. I cannot comment on female hockey players, let's just say that those girls who play up on the teams with boys will make fantastic CEOs someday. I am confident they'll figure out how to manipulate their male co-workers for fun and profit. Girls, I'm just saying: they are not that hard to figure out.

Our U13 team was very athletic and fast, the coach had found the "it" factor when selecting the team that year. These Colorado kids were training at high altitude and living on crappy carbs and Gatorade. As parents, we all knew what was happening: they were bonding like a little pack of wolves and started to develop their own language. We had a younger assistant coach named Grapes who helped them learn the wise ways of chirping and it was widely known that swearing properly was just as much of a skill as blocking a shot.

For those teams that stay together, these are the pre-billet years. Some of us had to drive one hour each way to the rink, spending thousands of dollars on gas and car maintenance over the years. I would often make plans with another mom and go for a walk, run to Target, or meet for coffee. Sometimes I would just sit in my car, looking at my phone and listening to true crime podcasts. I also picked up some work editing college essays for kids in S. Korea. Talk about random side-hustles. I learned that some families actually moved closer to the rink, selling their homes and transferring to a new school so that their kids could get a better night's sleep. Some even tried the online schooling options, but who knows how well that education translates to knowledge when it is time for college. Carpools, early dismissals, prepared meals in Tupperware were all part of the story. Do we still *say* Tupperware?

This is where my other kids started to squawk at my fervent food preparation for this one kid. I would make burritos, protein drinks and snacks for the road on top of making dinner for the rest of the family (yes, heating up leftovers counts). Hockey-boy got his own special meal for after school, the rest of the family had to eat leftovers or thaw frozen Costco food. In order to prepare for the hour-long road trip to practice, I put everything in foil and met him after school so I could drive him to dryland (off-ice workouts) and then onto the rink. My car smelled like a dumpster behind a Chinese restaurant. Sometimes I had to get his skates sharpened or pick up a new stick. My life ended at 2:45 pm every Monday-Thursday. Livin' the dream, bitchez!

However, on those long drives we talked about school, friends, homework, hockey and family. We listened to his music, then my music, then no music since one of us usually had a headache by that time. On carpool days, I was a chauffeur and enjoyed listening to the boys' conversations that centered on NHL draft picks, fantasy teams, even other sports mixed in with funny memes or videos they all knew about on YouTube. There were also some nasty-ass rap songs that I learned to love, definitely nothing I would sing out loud in front of my own mother without needing to go to confession.

In the early years, parents went to tournaments and stayed in the same room as their kids. My husband and I would alternate on tournament weekends as someone would need to stay home for the other kids and the dogs. It was on those plane trips, rental car pickups, using GPS to find restaurants, the rink, gas stations, pharmacies and local skate shops that we learned the essence of traveling for a sport. It didn't matter what town it was, we learned how to navigate and solve problems. It was an apprenticeship of sorts for him. For me, it was more like becoming his personal assistant. I would make up for it by torturing him with pump up songs from the '90s and recount every Michael Jordan story I knew, especially the one where he had the flu and played in game 5 of the NBA finals against the Utah Jazz. 38 points. Da Bulls!

These are the years that I would not trade for the world. On the one hand, you are bleeding money and time. On the other hand, you are setting an example on how to travel, how to treat people along the way, and how to be the one person in the world that a kid can count on. You get to know each other. Coaches come and go, advisors dip in and out, but the parent is the one that holds it together so the kid can thrive. This is the best part of the trip as sherpa. Bluebird skies for that part of the trek. I loved it and will forever cherish our time together.

That being said, I saw some parents lose their shit. If I had a dime for every time I saw "how not to be *THAT* parent," I would have made up the hockey deficit. Dads looking like they wanted to murder the coach, moms crying in the bathroom, kids looking like they were in trouble just by making eye contact with their parents after a "bad" game. We've all heard the nasty fans, the parents who get kicked out for yelling at the refs or starting fights with the other team's parents. For as much as we all love hockey, there are some deep scars and emotional reactions that are akin to a psychotic episode at every tournament. I've even witnessed a guy flashing his gun as a way to intimidate a wordy father. I hid in the bathroom on that one, after spending a summer in Washington D.C. in my twenties, witnessing a crime means you have to give police statements and go to court. Homey don't play that.

There is also the risk of fights on the ice that get ugly,

sometimes a kid uses his skate blade when another is down. On purpose. Other times it could be an accident, but severed carotid arteries can kill, and it happens enough that it scared the shit out of me. I cringed anytime I saw a player down and the kid who is just full of anger decides to suckerpunch and kick. I'm guessing there may have been a few rough car rides home over the years for *those* kids, perhaps some pent up anger and aggression. Could be a situation wherein a kid feels like the way they play is never "enough."

I wonder how many hockey kids go to juvie?

Our team also experienced a violent episode where the entire fan base of the other team (French Canadians, they're not always as nice as we think) threw things on the ice. Then they waited for the ref to leave so they could accost him. Half of their team and coaches got kicked out of the game. That tournament was highly competitive, it was great hockey to watch despite the mini-episode of Moms Gone Wild with Dick-Bag Dads.

Commercials, memes, podcasts all go after the parents on this stuff because it is sometimes true. Just when we think there's too much political rhetoric and violent home-grown extremists, we have the grownups in hockey. We ask the players to leave it all on the ice, so if you happen to be the CCM-hat angry hockey dad or the venomous tight-jean wearing botox babe, don't be surprised if down the road your kid is told they just aren't that good. But they could have been.

Eventually, the most insane behavior will settle down as the kid gets older. The better the team is, the less loud the parents are (except for Canadians, they don't have the same fear of USHL scouts like the USA Hockey kids do). Maybe there is something to be said for all that money and time together. It makes you realize that your behavior as a parent has a lot to do with how far your kid gets with the sport.

That said, I've seen social media posts by college scouts that admit to crossing a name off of their prospect list based on how the parents act. This is real, and it could affect your kid's future. Hockey, for as beautiful and violent of a sport that it is, does not welcome fury and vitriol from the parents. Essentially, this behavior is poison to the well of opportunities. Your kid will resent you. Period.

Navigation tip: Shut your piehole. If you can't say something nice, don't say it at all, or you could ruin your kids chances. Don't bang the glass either. Go lay down, meditate or watch Step Brothers. Don't get me wrong, there are some bad things that can happen off the ice and you need to be on alert. But when the game is being played, keep your murderous wishes and hexes on the team, other players or the coaches buried down deep in your gut, and take a Tums like the rest of us do.

By the time kids are in U14, they get to travel without the parents and instead move as a team with coaches and a team manager. This is the first time they get to be away from home as a unit and they enjoy every part of their independence from parental pressure. Early mornings (8 a.m.) are a bit strained, as the boys seem to be struggling to digest their breakfast and stay awake for the bus ride but they still manage to issue funny insults (a.k.a. "chirps") to one another that make even the most serious coach crack a smile. As they get older, they are much more inwardly focused, as they have probably had some mental sports coaching or an app that tells them how to breathe. Pre–game routines are all over the board. In these early teenage years, they're still just kids, not professional athletes. My son told me that ages 13-15 are the most fun of all the travel years.

I once heard a highly respected hockey coach tell parents that there are only a few questions you should ask your son/daughter after a game:

1. Did you have fun?
2. Were you a good teammate?
3. Where should we eat?

Great advice. It's easy to forget the simple things. I've seen parents huddle around their players after a good game, giving big hugs and celebrating the small stuff even if that kid hardly played. I've also watched kids peel off from the group to call their dad after a game, intense in their run-down on their individual performance. To each their own, everyone has their process. Offer what is needed and ensure that the kid is leading the process, not the other way around. There are books on "how to be a sports parent" and what not to do. Yeah, well...you decide what you want to read, nobody is perfect and everyone makes mistakes. Do the best you can. Remember, they have only one childhood.

I spoke to a former goalie once about why he left hockey after making it to the Quebec Major Junior Hockey League. He said that when he was 17, he fell in love with a girl. His father was so upset that she was taking away his focus on his game, so he did not allow him to date in the following hockey season. Eventually, he had a falling out with his dad and it took years to repair the relationship. Apparently, it was one particular Canadian Thanksgiving with the new wife, smokin' some darts out back and talking it out. Gramps made peace with his son, explaining that his actions were all from a place of love. Now Gramps wants to help coach his only grandson, promising that he won't say anything if he finds a girlfriend. Cue theme from Lion King right here. You can't unhear it, can you?

In the meantime, the kids will create their chirps as part of an unofficial creative writing stint, maybe some of these kids will be joke-writers for the next comedy sitcom or meme account. Arrested Development is on full display if you follow social media accounts whose content creators are no longer trying to get scouted. Examples of some great hockey chirps (these are PG-13) courtesy of comments on instagram @hockeybenders:

"Did you forget your skates and bring your clown shoes?"

"Does your coach know you're on the ice?"

"You are the best kid on the ice today!"

"Has your goalie ever tried dodgeball?"

"I've heard better chirps from a dead bird."

"Turn around."

"You're more useless than a white crayon."

"You've been dropped more times than the puck."

"I've seen better wheels on a canoe."

"Hey buddy, make me a sandwich."

"I've seen better hands on a digital clock."

"You're not very good at hockey, try soccer."

"I've seen better edges on a circle."

"Your mom is hot."

"Your sister is hot."

"Your goalie is so bad he couldn't save a Google doc."

"Aren't you on the 4th line?"

"You're so dusty a swiffer won't even go near you."

"You probably think hybrid icing is a soy-based cake topping."

One of my favorites is "Your mom liked my instagram post from 2 years ago."

There are a million more, one begets the next. It all depends on the heat of the moment and how good they are at the art of chirping.

7

THE PARENT FANDANGO

F andango is slang for nonsense and tomfoolery. There is no doubt this was the very definition of our U13, U14, and U15 year team parents. Not sure if the mothers had all taken extra potent prenatal vitamins, but these seasons for our birth year was the most fun for both kids and parents.

Navigation Tip: Be a nice person. These hockey parents can become your family if you treat them the way you want to be treated.

Maintain your humor and check any superiority complex at the door; it's your kid that has to prove themselves on the ice. That said, a hockey parent must survive a season full of awkward social settings, establishing that you are not a threat. Aside from rolling onto your back and peeing on yourself to prove it, just be nice. Be funny. Be unassuming and get to know the team parents. You don't have to find a new bestie or be the most popular, but you may find out that there is a lot to learn from the quieter parents who raised 5 hockey players. You will consume large amounts of caffeine together. You will get the same emails from the organization, specialty camps and scouting reports. Oh yeah, and if you're lucky enough to have a parent who also happens to be an orthopedic surgeon, buy them dinner early in the season.

Our team was a solid group of talented and athletic kids with passion and drive. Our coaches were both from Europe and had phenomenal backstories of how they made it up the ranks to the NHL. I won't use names but let's just say we had the best of the best in hockey knowledge for the skaters. Poor goalies, they never had anyone "famous" working with them, but that's sometimes the fate when you're a goalie. Goalies are in a different caste system, they need lots of private coaches and a different mental composition.

As to the characters in the parent group, the Dads dominated in earning the title of Fandango. As a posse, they each deserve their own chapter and I'm sure there are enough antics that could make a series out of this book, I'll let them decide if they want to me to ghost-write it for them. They'd probably market it as Volume Two of "We're Not Here fer the HOCKerrrrrssss" as they attempt to demonstrate their loogie-hocking prowess while snort-laughing and trying to make a putt with a lob wedge. Ironic, since almost every one of their sons went on to the juniors or college hockey so I can't say they weren't there for the hockey. But they did have shirts made up that said, "We're Not Here for the Hockey," and it is that shirt which inspired the title for the book.

"I mean, we're here *because of* hockey" one dad told me as he sported his tight T-shirt over the hoodie he was already wearing. They addressed each other by their last names, except for a few private nick-names that would come out when alcohol was involved. Imagine a hockey sitcom: Animal House meets Seinfeld. Add the moms who simulated Everyone Loves Raymond mixed with Bridesmaids, and a sprinkle of Hallmark Christmas specials, finished off with Pinterest snack ideas and team apparel. There were a few parents who did not participate in the Fandango for good reasons, it was never harped on but understood that they *were* there for the hockey, and did not want to end up on America's Funniest Home Videos or Cops.

The following is a pastiche of observations of many Parent Fandangos. Cue the Mexican Hat dance song right here, it'll set the mood.

You've seen the Parent Fandango groups in the hotel lobbies, circling around one end of the bar or on the couches with extra purchases of six packs and bourbon. The party was the reward for watching hockey without busting a blood vessel in your own eye. Everyone got along for the most part and supported each player on the team, regardless of skill or points. No hang ups, no hookups or swingers. I've heard that other teams had issues with drunk coaches never making it to the 8 am game, or a crazy mom who flashed her boobs to the group on a dare. Never happened in our group, we were too busy playing immature drinking games or singing Karaoke. Okay, maybe someone was blackout drunk and broke something, but I think she blamed it on another mom who was already in bed for the night. It's all good, they left a good tip.

All the kids on the team were from Colorado, and many of them grew up in the local leagues together. Most of this team had been to the Pee Wee tournament in Quebec, so they had traveled as a pack for a while. I was warned to avoid certain situations from a couple of parents before I even sipped my first beer. Their humor played off of one another regardless of the revolving door of dads whose sons left the team at some point. They drank, gambled, cheered, and provided a Wall of Hopes and Dreams as they stood together on the top bleachers, center ice. A few sat with their wives (rarely), a few paced or separated themselves at the end of a rink or served as penalty box volunteers. To each their own, nobody should judge that, it's all superstition, tolerance and how charged up your social battery is before a game. Or maybe they just don't like you.

At first, the core of the dads were intimidating. Bravely, I entered their circle to have a beer at the first tailgate and it seemed as if they tolerated my presence with a rated PG-13 version of their jokes. I quickly learned that wives were off getting Starbucks or sitting in each other's cars to stay warm and visit, so I did not make a practice of it and realized my husband really shined as he stepped up to earn a spot in the pre-game-male-only-Fandango. Clearly a fraternity, calling each other brother at first, only to be lambasted with a new name representing any missteps of drunken dares the night before. It was abundantly clear that these men needed to bond. This wasn't just a tailgate for a sporting event. This involved their own flesh and blood, the fruit of their loins. Belonging ensured entry into the tribe of warriors. It was primal and silly, good-natured and full of testosterone and middle-aged angst. It was actually a wonderful thing to witness. When one of their sons scored, there was a distinct look that washed over their faces. Pure joy and pride. As a kid, I remember one of my favorite parts of watching the Olympics was when the camera found the parents of the Olympians in the stands. It was that same expression, a very palpable emotion that all parents have when their kid makes them proud. When the good times ended, it was time to head back to reality, take out the garbage and go back to work on Monday.

The roller-coaster of feelings is difficult to explain to non-hockey parents. On some days, it feels like you forgot to buckle in, but the ride takes you upside-down anyway. It is thrilling and unexpected fun. You sometimes wish you had a scream pillow for the game. Sometimes you feel like you need to puke because of that icky-burning-feeling in your gut. Maybe something is going on in the locker room between the players. Perhaps the coach is riding your kid and it's not translating to any semblance of improvement. There are those total bummer game days and they are quickly replaced with ecstatic highs by the next game. Maybe your kid is on a line where a line-mate rarely passes, toe drags every time and is never corrected for being selfish. Or the defense pairing is a mess and rather than pass it properly, they ring the puck around the boards every time. There are so many scenarios because, over time, the feelings become more identifiable. More predictable. You build a tolerance to it, just like vodka. You could be so hopeful and jubilant in one period and by the third period, ready to crawl into bed and eat raw cookie dough.

Back to the roller coaster ride, some days it feels like you watched your wallet fall into the water on the loopty-loop you didn't see coming. That credit card bill is a few hundred bucks more this month because of new skates. Another stick. New dress shoes. They are always growing. All of these emotions are a direct extension of the journey your kid is on, but somehow you are accumulating all of the baggage. It gets heavier and heavier.

You live and die every minute your kid is out there on the ice. A 40-second shift can seem like too long for another line and not enough for your player's line. It's an eternity for a goalie parent. Your heart beats. You love it. Then you hate it. You love it. You hate it. Then you wonder if you are a psychopath.

I am here to offer you complicity in your manic bipolarity.

It is normal to feel like shit while trying to be happy for everyone else's kid that's having a good game. It is normal to hate the coach's decisions...and then love the coach's decisions. It is normal to have hockey-parent-syndrome where you think your kid deserves more. It is normal to not be happy for the kid that always scores. It is normal not to know how to act when your kid is having a scoring streak and people compliment you, as if you are responsible. You answer, "yeah....thanks.....he works hard" as you awkwardly simper. It is normal to feel guilty about overly celebrating when the kid who never scores gets a point, nobody likes to be patronized but you can't help it. It is normal to be annoyed by little kids running up and down the bleachers. Or by the guy that decides to stop and watch the game at the glass, blocking your view of the face-off. Maybe you are flying high because your kid played great, but they lost the game so you can't be too outwardly happy, as the goalie is probably having a crappy night. Emotions are unstable from August until mid-December. Feels like a short stint in rehab at Christmas, only to be thrust right back into it all by the first week in January through March. Or May. Or July. It just keeps going.

The hockey dads crave the back-slaps, bro-hugs and alcohol-induced shout-outs. The moms are into the communal hockey hugs and high-fives, but perhaps not always matching the bravado of the dads. However, there are plenty of times the moms silently implode anytime their kid gets Kronwalled by a defensemen, getting completely crushed into the boards and then skating off the ice holding their wrist or head. The Botox babes just yell out expressionless gasps, the others make sounds like sipping soup, clap and start talking to themselves until they know the kid is well enough to play the next shift.

There was one game where our local rivals (the Plan B team) were excessively chirpy and doing whatever they could to avenge their hockey pride. One of their skaters took a cheap shot and flattened our goalie after the whistle. It was a bench-clearing brawl resulting in both penalty boxes resembling small villages of hockey players. Or the impossible-to-win arcade claw game, the glass box filled with hockey boys instead of the crappy toys. Once we knew all the kids were still in one piece, the parents bonded over it. It was decidedly correct to applaud the skater getting kicked out of the game for unsportsmanlike conduct, then rewatch the video of the hit, and give the stink-eye to the rival Colorado parents on the way out of the rink. Like my kids tell me on ski days, there are no friends (or family) on powder days. Needless to say, there are no rival-team-friends on smash-our-goalie day, we'll catch up next time. Let's get together for happy hour soon!!!

Our team parents were lucky, it was a great group of people.

I have witnessed toxic team parents who were competitive as adults...and mean. Despite any "Parent Contracts" that are signed at the beginning of a season, there are always a few with axes to grind. The cliques were no different than a really bad after-school special with popular people being the jerks. This can be the organization's doing, the coach's favoritism of just a few players and their parents, or just a few assholes who spoil it for everyone. Overall, we were lucky as the majority of characters balanced one another out. It took some work on everyone's part to create that environment.

Without question, our team played well together because the parents played well together. Yes, we had a team mooch with a contentious divorce, often the butt of the jokes, but harmless in the long run. He was socially bludgeoned periodically, and deserved it.

Here's a quick accounting of some All-Star parent moments:

- The parent who, without hesitation, drove back to the hotel to pick up the missing jersey or extra skate for someone's else's kid.
- The parent who drove another mom to pick up her car that had been towed somewhere in Philly.
- The parent who hosted the mass sleepover because they lived closest to the rink in order to save the 4:30 am wakeup time for the parent who lives one hour away.
- The car-pools to practice, to and from airports, to local games.
- The unquestioning and unabashedly generous spirit of picking up the lunch tab for the kid who forgot their own money or lost their wallet on the plane.
- The kid who had pink-eye and the mom who got the prescription 40 minutes away from the hotel while the other moms personally changed the sheets and got extra towels for the roommate who didn't want to catch it.
- The driving to the hockey shops for a new stick, sharpening skates, special meal runs for the extra hungry kid.
- The trip to the ER to get a collar bone checked out, the broken wrist, the sprained shoulder or knee.
- Helping to cure the sinus infections, the coughs, the colds (pre-Covid, you played through your fevers!)
- Helping find the space in a hotel conference room for the quiet kid who needed time to decompress or do their homework.

- Delivering the team meals, buying more snacks and getting ice for the wounded, Band-aids and cough medicine for anyone that needed it.

Good people, good parents.

Navigation tip: There is a bit of quid pro quo in hockey. If you are counting on everyone else to drive your kid to practice or forget to reimburse the parent who picks up the tab for your kid who never remembers their wallet, you better be the volunteer who runs the clock or keeps score when the email comes out looking for said volunteers. You get a little bit of slack but don't be surprised when you don't get the invite to the next post-game chicken wings and dart tournament. The Fandango will turn on you.

A bit like the movie Gremlins, just add alcohol and some post-game euphoria (stress) and you have yourself a Parent Fandango at the team hotel. The stories, the laughter, the games all spearheaded by a few of the hockey dads that were getting their second chance at college parties. Let the wild rumpus begin!

There were some loose boundaries around releasing stress as a spectator. All hockey teams have a set of parents who know how to party. This is where the adage "what happens in Vegas stays in Vegas" applies to any out-of-town tournament. We had our characters who stirred the pot. Depending on the mix, there were a few tournaments where some parents got their panties in a knot and avoided the vulgarity of what could be best be compared to an old Howard Stern radio broadcast spiced with South Park humor and a Jackass finish.

There was one dad who was fantastic at creating drinking games. He could come up with a way to bet on anything, a maestro of initiating and instigation. The man could drink hard liquor like Don Draper of Mad Men, and yet stay in the zone of creating the next challenge. He must have watched a lot of Price is Right as a child but with an appetite for gambling. Rarely did I ever see him be a sloppy drunk. Shut up liver, you're fine.

There was a small group within this group that probably lost and won thousands of dollars over the course of a season. I'm not sure if anyone has a bookie shaking them down to this day, all I know is that I played a few rounds of trunk dice, rolling the hotel macrame balls down a table, Right-Left-Center, beer tab in the bucket and whatever else resembled a Bozo bucket game. I never won. Our coach played with the parents but he rarely lost, he was unbeatable. I remember reading about Tiger Woods in the book "Relentless: From Good to Great to Unstoppable" by Tim Grover. The professional athlete CANNOT lose. It's not in their mindset to lose, they keep playing until they win. Always with grace but mostly the eye of the tiger. You could see it, the narrowing of the pupil and the intensity of focus. They may lose a round or two of pool, but ultimately they won the final pot of crumpled up dollar bills.

Fortunately, our GenX dads were not big on posting social media, but did have some incriminating photos of those who had passed out in a bathroom or lounge chair of the lobby. Allegedly they had been roofied once by a visiting team. There were some torn hamstrings from foot races, AirBnB's in Toronto who kept the security deposits, drinking dares involving vodka with a live fish in the glass, a fork stuck in someone's arm, and a few busted tables from a beer pong game that resulted in a final match between the Iron Curtain descendants v. Democracy (the Reds won by the way).

When games were out of state, we always had families with relatives at home who wanted to watch the game. Despite the fact that there are media companies who charge a monthly fee for the live feed of games, our team demanded the free version. It no longer exists, but that medium was Periscope which was eventually replaced by Facebook Live. Getting people to volunteer was like asking someone to give up a kidney. I did it a few times. Think NPR story on how to make pfeffernusse cookies. Boring. I managed to play "name that tune" while turning the lens to the rafters, horrible commentary on what was happening, losing the puck and filming my crotch. Not fun. Every excuse in the book from "my phone is about to die" to "I don't have my glasses" to "I'm hungover too" were not good enough reasons. Someone had to do it.

Regardless of the medium, we fortunately had a dad whose color commentary will live in posterity. It was difficult to recruit anyone else once he became the voice of our team. In fact, people from the opposing teams would log into our feed while they were watching the game just for entertainment. His ability to call out the players on the line, say the play and in between the whistles make up stories about the parents of the player who was on the ice. If a kid got a penalty, he would say "there's an example of bad parenting."

Some of my favorites were:

- Oooh, that's gotta hurt. Jonesy just sent that puck, that goalie got it in the grapes. Ouch.
- So, I believe the opposing team's goalie is wearing some Serta mattresses on his legs. Special mention to our sponsor, Serta mattress for providing their product placement at today's game.
- Looks like player #21 is an adult male with a lip sweater. Nice mustache, they must feed these Minnesota boys raw meat with plenty of hormones for breakfast. I'll have my assistant producer check on that player's birth certificate and report back, not sure he's aware this is a youth hockey game. Nice MinneFLOWTA on the other defensemen in that pairing though. Shout out to Pantene, although his dad is sporting a skullet so enjoy that hair while ya got it buddy!
- Mark's dad just got back from kayaking in the Amazon, boy does he have some stories to tell. I believe a piranha got his right testicle during an unfortunate swimming accident, but looks like he's going to be ok. His wife has been a little grumpy lately.

- Jimmy's mom just returned from her keynote presentation at the UN recently, she's doing a great job at disarming the nukes in North Korea. I believe she can speak 5 languages, we'll need her out here soon to help us figure out what the Canadians are yelling aboot. What language do they speak in Montreal? Wait, *THAT'S* French?
- Looks like my son is a bit lost, trying out some of his figure skating skills at the moment, that edge work is fantastic. God bless him, how much did we pay for lessons?
- Looks like Zach broke another stick. This tournament just got even more expensive. I see his dad crying in the corner, someone get that man a beer!
- Looks like we got Danny wheeling around the net like a Nascar driver, making eye contact with several of his teammates but nowhere near where the puck needs to go. Meanwhile Teddy is sitting wide open at the net, looking like he could have a lunch break there, waiting for a pass. And there's the whistle, and somehow we lost the puck.
- There's a nice pass, and another pass, there's a shot, there's a rebound and another pass...nobody home, and the other team has gained control of the puck. Looks like there's a disagreement between the coach and Stripes on that one, not sure what the call is but my guess is that they are having a nice debate over whether it's too early for pumpkin spice. And our team has another penalty, definitely there's some bad parenting going on here. Really bad parenting.

It was incredibly funny and self-deprecating. If grandparents made comments online from home, he would respond. He would also take "fan" films during the breaks, having conversations with the parents and odd spectators online who just "found" the game. It was perhaps the best way to enjoy hockey if you could not be there. Humor is a great way to relieve stress.

Needless to say the livestreaming kept us connected in an

otherwise very stressful "seat" when home. All of our parents were engaged in the team's success, we all loved it and supported it and each other. The occasional grumpy parent knew if they needed to extricate themselves, it was normal that everyone had a bad day at some point. The group did not tolerate nay-sayers, and we quickly learned that how YOU acted determines how many dinners you go to with the team parents. You may not find out where the "party" is after the game.

Navigation tip: Find a friend on the team whose player is in a different position.

If you have a forward, get the friend whose kid plays defense. Not sure what goalies do here, my guess is that they are eternally damned to live in a private hell since they always have distinct and separate gripes that skater parents cannot possibly understand. Maybe the other goalie was simpatico, but not really. When your forward works well with another defensemen and maybe they have that special something, you can talk to that parent about your happy moments, grudges, or misgivings but always with arms length. No guarantees, just have to be sure you can live with it if it gets out.

In any case, this mom or dad will pump your tires when yours are flat, will commiserate with you all under the blood pact that you cannot undermine their trust, tell their secrets in any way shape or form, or say anything negative about their kid. Once you have that trust, it is a bond as strong as the one you have with your personal belief that somehow you are still a person outside of hockey. The great thing about this friend is that he or she will listen to your concerns, your fears, your sense of injustice for your son because they often have it going on as well. Everyone needs someone to hear them out and talk them out of their tree. The season gets so emotional, so out of proportion to what "else" is important in life, that this friend will lend their hand to you, pulling you out of the quicksand that has become your hockey alter ego. Or just hire a really good therapist.

Hockey parents generally shine in the sympathy department, offering support through the loss of a loved one, an injury, a kid who gets cut at tryouts, health issues of a parent - the families become your family. Even when something happens to a player (car crashes, house fire, etc) and you learn about it online or through some other medium, total strangers will chip in for that family. Hockey is generous, families know how to step up when it matters the most.

To this day, the hockey moms from the teen years get together for movies, little getaways, and group chats. We keep in touch and root for one another, many of us empty-nesters now and in some cases, traveling all over the country and Canada to watch their sons pursue the next level. The Parent Fandango title is still held by the core group of dads, getting together for a golf tournament or to watch an NHL game at someone's house or playing pool at a bar. Group chats to keep up and especially to congratulate a college commit or scoring streak of one of their players.

The Fandango endured and shined in what could have been considered a golden age. However, all good things must come to an end. Pavel, the head coach for the past three years, was ready to relinquish the reins. The organization had appointed a new coach for the U16 season and his preference was to separate from the parents. The new head coach was coming in hot for our team, ready to strategize new systems and provide a different discipline on the bench.

The newly appointed head coach believed that the U16 year should be used as a preparation year for what was next in hockey. The next level meant playing juniors, with hopes of the USHL, NAHL, WHL or BCHL[1] leagues and eventually NCAA[2] and/or the NHL. This was the mission statement outlined in the beginning of the season. Seemed like the most professional way to define expectations. As parents, we all agreed with these edicts and were hopeful this guy knew what he was doing. He was fairly new to coaching competitive youth hockey.

A few of our U15 players had played up on his team the year before and were prepared for his coaching style. We knew that he had strong opinions about certain players, some good and some not so good. I noticed a bit of backbiting, perhaps envy, shrouded in flattery for Pavel's achievements. This is a parody version, of what we seemed to hear:

Hear ye, Hear ye. I have a proclamation to make. I will arrive at my new domain soon...

and at my command, dutiful subjects who desire to make it to the next level will indeed make it to the next level by following my systems and forgetting all of what they know as their strengths, I will decide their strengths... as I see them to be undisciplined, I mean, Pavel did a great job with them.....they are mine to mold under my tutelage. I will soon be able to take the credit...I mean, get them noticed...Rock music will play and pageants will take place. Bear ye well these facts in mind. Behold, me.

Just like scouts watch a player's body language, I noticed the Parent Fandango cringe, appearing wide-eyed and nervous. A few went into a sycophantic response, preferring to smile and compliment him as if they wanted the new teacher to know their son was not a troublemaker. The familial banter stopped in his presence and parents went into the best professional version of themselves, as if everyone was on high alert. There was a new sheriff in town and he was ready to make changes for the sake of making changes.

When the season started, we learned later that many of the players felt it was the worst they had ever felt about playing hockey because of the coach's strange antics and head games. Classic case of arrested development, many of us felt a sense of dread before each tournament. However, it seemed to unify the bunch in the name of brotherhood. They still gathered in the locker room 30-45 minutes earlier than they needed to. Misery loves company, and they had a common cause - to play for each other, nobody was alone. All for one and one for all.

A few boys stepped up to navigate the coach's mood swings, often saying the right things to keep the peace. They knew the risk of pissing him off could mean a bad review for the next interested scout.

The captain took the major hit as he was the yes-man and responsible for keeping order amongst friends he had since he was 7 years old. He was the perfect kid to play the role: stoic, respectful, wise, and silently leading his troops through a pandemic year of hockey. For him, it was fantastic practice for becoming a top notch hedge fund manager someday.

Maybe that was the coach's master plan all along? Maybe they needed to spend a week in the woods together. For certain kids, any vulnerability was pounced upon and left a nice mental mess for the parents to deal with. Many of the families said they did not want to fly out for the games because of travel restrictions and positive Covid tests. That was a great excuse. The Parent Fandango was no longer a nomadic tribe but rather a loose gathering of straggling parents in the lobby of a home game or outside for a pickup game of bags. The ritual of supporting the team just wasn't fun anymore. Grumblings amongst the families were kept quiet, nobody officially complained and just coached their sons to get through the season, focusing on the bigger picture. I remember advising my own son, "keep your head down, do what he says, agree and suck-it-up....it's part of life."

My son mentioned that hockey felt like a job. A career choice. Not much creativity or fun. This had nothing to do with lack of passion, grit or skill but everything to do with the coach's hard-on for power trips, as they were told "this is how it is" in juniors. Whether it's a coach, a boss, or quite possibly a family member, there is always someone that knows how to put the fun in dysfunctional. Or maybe the diss in dysfunctional?

Playing hockey through a pandemic was strange for all of us and it seemed the stress was wearing on the coach. It seemed to many of us that his reactions to parent questions was misguided and that he would take it out on the team. But then he'd buy the players things, treat them to outings to make up for it. It didn't seem right to me. It was a great cover for what otherwise could be described as insidious mind-fucks.

It was a challenging time. I decided to nickname him The Agitator. He had a whiff of characteristics similar to the coach in the

2014 movie called Foxcatcher where Steve Carrell plays a multimillionaire megalomaniac. In our version of that movie, the coach undermined the athletes' motivation by fixating on certain players who seemed to serve his own psychological needs. This coach lasted just one season at this level despite the fact that our team made it to the final game of Nationals which they would have anyway.

Sour grapes? Nah, not anymore, but if you had asked many of the parents how we felt in those days, we would have happily traded him.

Time heals all wounds and the painful memories will be replaced with the good ones. The Parent Fandango revived and is just as snarky as ever. A few kids bowed out after that season who could have gone on. Who knows if the grind and the scathing comments got the best of them? On a positive note, the value of having hockey during a pandemic was that the players all managed to blow off steam by ridiculing all of it in their group chats or locker room talks. At the end of the day, the player has to endure some bad days in a season. The last time I checked, a hockey coach is not required to have an advanced degree in child psychology.

Navigation Tip: Be prepared for emotional fallout.

Not every "mean" coach is bad. In fact, someone who yells but also corrects and keeps discipline on the bench is great preparation for the next level in life, whether they play hockey or not. Watch out for abuse that's hyper-focused or tearing down a kid for fun or some sick need to prove a point for himself. We give these types of coaches too much power as they also can be vindictive and call prospective colleges or junior teams to inform them that the player is not fit for the next level, under the guise of having character flaws. This type of clandestine activity sometimes has to do with loyalty (wanting to play for a different team) or the kid just doesn't take the abuse, making eye contact rather than subservience. It happens in many sports, it sucks, and in some cases, those coaches don't come back. This is ultimately a problem of the organization and they should do better, unless the organization is too busy counting cash. In the meantime, stay up to speed on changes in your athlete's behavior, signs of burnout or lack of motivation in school. It should be noted that in some situations, those kids that weather the storms manage to move on to Division I hockey. There's always a silver lining somewhere, just need to look up.

I found a great speech online by John Kessel as he was being inducted into the American Volleyball Coaches Association Hall of Fame, "Never Be a Child's Last Coach." The quagmire in hockey is that hockey players have humility which keeps them from blaming anyone other than themselves, but eventually, they find ways to overcome (by quitting or moving on). So if the standards are "don't be THAT parent," how about some customer satisfaction surveys for those coaches that go unchecked? Just a suggestion, my liege.

Hockey can pick the scabs of deep-seeded, ugly emotions. Not everyone cares about your kid or where they are at the moment. As a parent, it can sometimes feel like you don't have anyone outside the family to talk to about it with. It can be heartbreaking. This is where it's important to have respect for the extended hockey family and lean into it. Your team parents are also part of the collective experience that is going to shape your son or daughter's perspective in life. This ethos is very important and as part of the parent group, you are setting an example. Oh yeah, it's time to Adult. Hard, but you can do it. Remember, you are a parent first, fan second. Hopefully you have a good Parent Fandango somewhere along the line.

You're not always there for the hockey.

8

THE RINKS AND THE RATS

O n a lighter note, let's talk about ice rinks.

Our home practice rink was ancient, only the Canadian teams who traveled to play us respected it for what it was. The place was a pit, always five times colder than any other ice rink. The floorboards under the player's bench were rotten wood, the ice had holes at the boards, the area under the bleachers was a mix of full-grown rabbit sized dust bunnies, lone gloves, empty cups and used Kleenex. If you dropped something through the bleachers, you would immediately scream "NOOOO" and ask some random little brother of a player to retrieve it for you. We were all well-trained to bring the bare minimum, since if you dropped a cell phone or purse, you would need a hazmat unit to disinfect it. Or more likely just leave it where it lay because, to quote the movie Sandlot, "It's gone, man. Gone."

The bathrooms had the mirrors they use at highway rest stops, reflecting a funhouse version of your face. The stuff you see in nightmares, sometimes a light bulb was flickering and you'd swear you could see the ghost of hockey mom past, staring at you with bags under her eyes. The grout holding the toilets in place had been sloppily fixed, apparently by a 5-year old with a can of whipped cream. The bench-style seats in the lobby were one foot off the ground, so if Grandpa sat on it accidentally, he'd require a knee replacement if he stood up too fast. There were dented vending machines for Gatorade, junk food and a water fountain to refill the water bottles.

The kids loved it. No reason to complain, if anything it was a source of pride to come from such humble beginnings. You left the rink always feeling "dirty" like you would after a day at an amusement park or a crowded airport. I tried to block out thoughts of E-coli and MRSA as the boys had the responsibility of keeping their locker room "clean" - this simply meant that food wrappers and used sock tape and empty disposable water bottles needed to be thrown out periodically. They were allowed to leave their bags there overnight to "air out" equipment and practice jerseys. Yes, please circulate the swass! Even if it's dry, it is still very pungent. To be fair to the boys, the aroma of mom's yoga pants after a sweaty vinyasa class are just as gamy. *For those who need the definition of swass, it's the sweat found around a person's ass crack. Sweat + ass = swass.*

There is no perfect way to describe the way a locker room for hockey players actually smells. When I was in college, I took a biology class that described a behavior that certain animals exhibited after smelling the urine or privates of another animal: the "flehman grimace."[1] It's when a horse or a goat gets a whiff of a certain scent and curls back their upper lip, exposing the front teeth. That's how our faces look when they open that door. There is always a stench that cannot be bleached away. Maybe I'll try making a candle out of it. A little ass smell infused with Axe body spray and bleach. Trust me, someone would buy it.

The boys had their rituals, the banter and the decompression, the humor and the continuous line of chatter was what drew them to practice 30-45 minutes early. This group, like many other competitive teams, loved to refer to their rituals as FERDA.

FERDA boys is something a mom is not really allowed to say, we sound stupid referencing it. Kinda like if a grown man told his teenage daughter that he knows how she feels when she gets her period. Just don't even try.

For the purposes of this book, though, I get to say it because I heard it all the time. It comes from Letterkenny, a Canadian sitcom.

Saturdays are FERDA Boys. That's it! Just a way to acknowledge that this space is for them to be sweaty, be themselves and not hide behind any other social expectations that they have in middle or high school. Their hockey personality is not the same representation of themselves that people know and understand in school or at home or in church. They are allowed to be rude, funny, loud, quiet, postured for a fight, ready to defend, ready to pounce. Getting pushed over while getting dressed or locker slammed when least expecting it is a way for adrenaline, hormones, rejection from girls, expectations from dads, worrying from moms, and other insecurities to disappear. This place was holy ground. It goes without saying that not everyone is always a true part of it. There are the boys who make the team because the coach needed a fourth line. Sometimes those boys know their role and are okay with it. Just eternally hoping to fit in with the banter, avoiding any below the belt comments referring to their "being good" or not. My guess is that they'd rather have a third nipple and get made fun of over that than being called bad at hockey.

The banter of the core of the group, and the mutual respect of being on a good team, gave these boys an overall expectation of themselves to move on to the next level of their sport. They drove each other to strive for excellence. The boys were always buzzin' during their warmups, a palpable sense of joy and excitement for their collective well-being.

Like clockwork, in January and February, the flu went through our team like pinkeye at a daycare. Someone had a sore throat, fever and a cough and then one by one, they'd fall into the common cesspool of germs. Vomiting usually stopped spreading after one or two kids, thankfully, because it's hard to skate while puking. On the drive home, cracking the window for fresh air was my only defense from their hacking coughs that were brewing new hockers, only to be spit out the back window on the highway or onto an unsuspecting cyclist.

Our ice rink was ground zero for viruses. The rink rats were always sick. Based on the low humidity and close quarters in the locker room and on the bench, it would be a fortunate accident if they didn't get sick more than twice in a season. 4-5 times was common. The kids that were more susceptible to "lung disease" had multiple inhalers. At one point, two boys each had to have their lungs scraped, only to discover bacterial infections that needed to be manually sucked out. Gross.

None of us really know if the hazards of an old ice rink show up later in life, but one can only hope that the high-energy nature of heavy breathing while full-out skating expelled any living organisms from the lungs. Many times these boys stayed in an anaerobic state for the last 5-10 seconds of their shifts and did that multiple times per day. At high altitude.

Most of us had apothecary versions of Mary Poppins' bag filled with cough drops, Robitussin, Nyquil, Prednisone, Albuterol, ibuprofen, and honey lemon cough drops on reserve from January to May. Kids were used to drinking Emergen-C all season long. Then there was foot fungus, which could be avoided by wearing shower shoes but those who already had it just went barefoot and sprayed antifungal powder directly into their socks and skates. Basic good hygiene practices flew out the window. I propose that superbugs can be killed by taking a hockey kid's sweat and making a vaccine out of it. We should ask Pfizer to take a look at it, maybe it's the cure for the forever-flu. Could help fund the next generation of AAA superhumans.

Cold or flu. Pulled hamstring or sore shoulder. Concussion. Bloody lips. MCL strain. ACL strain. Broken collarbone. Injury and illness all go with hockey. A mantra handed down by Grapes (the younger assistant coach) was: "You're fine." Eventually it caught on with the parents: one mom had a hip replacement and her son said,

"You're fine." When Covid started to pick off the players one by one, the collective response was simply "You're fine." At some point, I considered having it tattooed on my own wrist, as it seemed to sum up the Zen of Hockey: nothing really matters and nobody cares.

Navigation Tip: You're fine.

9

PLAYING TEAM MANAGER

In the eyes of the Vatican, there are 5 steps to being ordained as a saint. If you agree to be a team manager, there are only three.

Step 1: Become a servant of the team and whipping post for the organization

Step 2: Show proof of heroic virtue

Step 3: Perform miracles

I am not a saint, by any means, but I served in this role for two years when my son played Bantam level (U14 and U15). Sausage and laws, best not to watch how they are made. Same with managing travel sports. It's brutal and you'll wish for the innocence of being a spectator parent.

Travel Tip for Team Manager: Get your boarding pass, find a row close to the front, then turn your back to oncoming traffic. Start rifling through your bag, have enough "stuff" to unpack and repack and people will pass by your row because you are emitting a sense of "you don't want to sit near me, I'm a hot mess." Once your hockey friend comes along, voila! You are instantly ready to sit and start the process of settling into what will be a stressful weekend. Nothing but smiles, nerves and excitement. And your own row.

~

As a team manager, you should be able to get into the express lane when it's time to go to heaven. Put it this way, at the end of the season, if the team gives you a better gift than the coaches, you did it! You accept the job because you want to help, and volunteering is part of your role as a parent.

They reel you in by offering to cover your hotel, plane ticket and food. It is a significant cost savings if you prefer to see live hockey. When someone asks you to volunteer for team manager, ask questions and be ready to commit a large portion of your day to hockey-related emails, planning and administrative tasks. It depends on how actively involved your coaches are and how much authority you really have. You may want to interview other hockey manager veterans as part of your decision making, as every organization is different. Most likely, they will openly discuss the suckiness of the role, but for some reason they are doing it for the 2nd or 3rd year in a row. Not me: two years was one year too long. I still remember being asked to do it again for the second year. I hesitated, but my apprehension was overcome by flattery. Sucker! You know that look on a doctor's face when they have bad news? The reality is they are going to try and give you the news with an optimistic treatment plan. Yes, you have a peculiar looking mole, we need to get it biopsied and sent to a lab. It could be precancerous, but these things are treatable. Cajolery, you're fine.

If you are considering taking the role as team manager, just know it's pretty darn close to all-consuming. It's a full-time job, maybe part-time if you split it with another parent. You get to see all of your kid's games and the team buys your carb-loaded food! It's what real sherpas eat! This is where you should negotiate a personal trainer to help you body-build. You get to stay in the hotel with the team. Here's a thought, maybe negotiate getting all the hotel points for the rooms as a Christmas bonus. For some, this seems like an automatic "win" because the price of traveling for hockey is exorbitant. Travel for one parent is roughly $1K per tournament, so if you are going to have 10 out of state tournaments, that's some really nice beach vacation money or perhaps a used car.

I had heard some stories about team managers who were in it for the wrong reasons, namely getting in with the coaches' circle. I never wanted to be accused of having an ulterior motive, so I decided that my persona could be a professional organizer with unflappable control. I strived to maintain an err of neutrality. I had heard of stories of managers changing score sheets, gossiping and back-stabbing. I didn't want to be that person.

Fortunately, I had coaches who were hands-off and gave me a lot of leeway to get shit done. There was an unwritten rule that I ran the business of hockey so they could focus on coaching and winning the tournaments. Yeah yeah, it's all about development, but ex-NHL coaches want to win. They are hard-wired and know what it takes because it is a natural flow from their professional career. No such thing as rolling the lines anymore, the players knew it when they tried out. The nice thing about a coach raised in the decades from Cold War era Europe is that they don't mince words. Teamwork is important– but you need to play with instinct and jell. Be creative. Adapt. Here are the rules, let's look at the board, now execute. Finish. Don't let your foot off the guy's neck as you are drowning him. Annihilate. Don't hold back. Feelings don't matter, don't be soft. Play the game. Get out of your head.

As a team manager, I was willing and able to accept this supportive role to both the organization and the coaches. I had to convince myself that it didn't matter if my son wasn't playing on the first line, or didn't see a power play opportunity every game or got skipped in overtime. As a team player, you learn to bury your emotions deep into your gut and coat the budding ulcer with late night ice cream and a Tylenol P.M. It wasn't easy; I may have cracked a few times.

Navigation Tip: Have multiple phone chargers. Packable blanket. First aid kit with extra ibuprofen. Good shoes. Warm hat. Tito's vodka.

~

Boston, 2018: First tournament without parents, the kids were U14. As a mother of a player, I was the only parent (aside from the coach) on the team flight and in the hotel. I had the discussion with my son that I would do my best not to embarrass him, but no promises. If you choose to do this job, your son must have enough comfort with you being around but also a thick skin because inevitably some part of your anatomy will be part of a running joke. In my case, I have a mom-version of a J-Lo butt. It *is* hard to miss, I have been known to knock over a toddler or two in my time just by turning around. If I played hockey, I would always be off-sides. Bending over near or around the team was prohibited, as I knew which kids were the instigators of the original observation of the size and shape of my ass. It was a source of bullying for me starting in the 5th grade, but thankfully Sir Mix-a-Lot and pop culture's subsequent never-ending homage to glorifying a big booty was my saving grace.

Needless to say, 14 and 15 year old boys are stupid funny. I finally succumbed to the fact that my own sense of humor calcified at that age. Farts are funny, talk about puberty related issues and man boobs was rated PG-13 at that age. Some boys were already getting hairier so the conversation could switch from "you're a potato" to something horrifying in about 3 seconds. Having already raised two teenage sons, I was thick-skinned. Nothing fazed me, but I certainly never relayed the transcript to any mother who asked me how their son behaved on these trips.

The first meetup at the Southwest bag drop was nerve-wracking. The coaches (Pavel and Lukas) and I were now responsible for 18 teenagers that had never traveled without their parents on a hockey tournament. As to "hoping" for a best case scenario, I shifted into middle-school gym teacher mode. I never had a whistle, just a loud mom voice. Something along the lines of "BOOOOYSSSS. PLEASE STAY ON THIS SIDE OF THE ROPE, GET YOUR BAGS OUT OF THE WALKWAY, PUT YOUR STICKS IN THE STICK BAG. FACE

FORWARD, BE READY, WATCH YOUR LANGUAGE THERE ARE
CHILDREN."

Translation: don't be an idiot.

Then they'd get their boarding passes and start heading into
security. It's great when they think it's funny to swap them with a
friend, especially if they have Russian last names. That caused a blip
in the line at security. Once they scattered and spent their parent's
cash on airport food, the boarding process became the next hurdle.
Luckily, there are group chats to herd the little darlings. Someone is
always off on their own quest for Smashburger or charging their
phone at another gate, but eventually they all line up.

Pre-Covid, it was like watching baby lion cubs. They roll around
and into any teammate, take little verbal jabs and push each other
into the next blob of boys. They have braces, greasy hair, pimples,
smelly armpits and dumb chirps. At this age, they are completely
unaware of their individuality because they all have one thing that
binds them together and it is their "equality" at this phase of life and
that keeps them grounded. Nobody is "better" than anyone in a
lineup at Southwest, there are no parents nipping at their heels
telling them to stand up straight or tuck in their shirts. They are
completely in a place of vulnerability. Their bodies have a concoction
of testosterone, Gatorade and Chipotle fueling their word choices.
Their banter and excitement for their first trip without parents
reflects that of a little boy who dreams of the NHL but still plays
Pokemon GO and orders the kid's meal.

The flight attendants usually give up on trying to order them
according to boarding pass number because if you are a good team
manager, you do one of two things: (1) remember to check-in 24 hours
before boarding to get them the "B" boarding so the entire line is your
kids, or (2) shit, you forgot and they all got "C" so you politely ask the
gate gods if they would consider boarding the boys first, sending
them to the back of the plane. You may argue that it's best for
everyone, it keeps them out of the way, they smell, and other
passengers will appreciate not having to sit near or between them.
This sometimes works and the rest of the plane is delighted when

they realize they have the front half of the plane to choose from. Glad that law school education of mine paid off.

Arriving at the Boston airport was an experience, I can still remember watching the herd of boys walking through the terminal like a little gray army. So proud of themselves, some darting off to the right in a race to pee quickly so as not to miss the procession. I am amazed by the ability of men to have the plain anatomical upper hand when it comes to urinating in a public restroom. To have the talent to run, pee in an open urinal en masse and run out of a public restroom and join up with the crowd all under 60 seconds.

As we waited for our bags, there was the mandatory conversation:

> I hope the stick bag didn't get lost because without sticks, you can't play...and that bag is probably worth over $15K....How many sticks did you bring? Two....Three? Goalie, how 'bout you, how many do you have?...whew...that's a lot of money and I wonder where a hockey store is near the rink... and did everyone get their skates sharpened before the tournament?... Does anyone see the team bag because that has all our pucks and extra jerseys and medical kit and...where did Jake go, did he go to the bathroom ...CaCaw! CaCaw!

And the boys respond..."what are we eating for dinner" and "I think I forgot my elbow pads" and "how far is it to the hotel" and "did we get a bus?" "Where do we need to go for the bus? And "what time is our first game?" And "who is my roommate again?" And "I may have left my wallet on the plane."

Needless to say, wear your hockey mom flak jacket because you'll feel like you're getting shot at. I would imagine myself as Willem Dafoe in Platoon, 1986, where he plays Sgt. Elias getting shot from behind. You go down, you get up, go down, reach forward, fall down, get up, but in this case, you have to stay standing. You're not a Vietnam soldier, just a hockey team manager.

Meanwhile, you look down at your cell phone to find about 10 texts from the parent who found their kids elbow pads in the garage and wondering how I was going to solve that problem. Maybe a text from your own family wondering if there is an extra house key somewhere because the garage door won't open. If you're lucky, you're playing everything off as if this is perfectly sane and normal. You've got this. You're fine.

We decided that buses were too expensive and that renting two 15-passenger vans plus a cargo van for all the equipment would save the team about $4K. So you pull up your mom jeans and tell the boys they need to stay in one place for a few minutes while we "get the vans." On that trip, Pavel and Lukas were first time travel companions outside of playing professionally together. They would alternate speaking in their native language and English, but for the most part I was enamored by their friendship. I was always a Blackhawks fan, so if my coach was Patrick Sharp I would have had a harder time not turning into a smitten 13-year old girl. Pretty sure I'd have a hard time making eye contact with those gorgeous eyes without blurting out "I love you." These guys were more like younger brothers to me. They were fresh off of playing professionally, had sons of their own and were ready to enjoy passing the torch to the next generation of players.

So we went to the Enterprise counter and pulled out the Costco Travel confirmation number. They signed their names, handed over their licenses, and got their keys. Due to the fact that cargo vans have a separate liability attached, we then drove to an off-site lot in a sketchy back alley near the airport to pick up the cargo van. That was my job, but I'd never driven anything larger than a minivan. Yikes. I was not going to succumb to being a weak helpless woman, so I confidently adjusted my --- wait, there is no rear-view mirror or camera? Crap....okay, only side mirrors. Why are the vents blowing freezing cold air on me? How do I turn the country station off? A few masked panic attacks and I noticed the coaches took off in the passenger vans. I realized real quick that these guys were racing one another and there was no way they were going to notice my hesitation. So, I put my GPS back on for the 2 mile trip back to the airport while receiving about 10 texts from my son who had become the team spokesman to find how much longer they had to wait.

As we pull up to the terminal, we find a large mound of bags with boys and phones all intermingled like nightcrawlers in a bait cup, freshly packed for fishing. There is some pushing and shoving as they spot us coming, and of course someone inevitably gets too close to the curb, so I slam on my brakes and get my first dose of adrenaline from being this badass hockey mom who can drive a cargo van with two ex-NHL players! I'm fucking cool!

As I jumped out of the driver's seat, careful not to make my debut as a badass hockey team manager with a yard sale fall, I opened up the back doors, which flew open with force. I was feeling strong and empowered. I put my 5'2" frame in front of the team, explaining that you can't just throw your bag in because they all need to fit. So after about 3 bags I realize that my words were nothing more than spit in the wind as about six bags block the ability of any more to go in, so I open the side doors and maybe two kids (who will make the best dads someday) rise to the challenge and start putting the bags in so they can all fit. The others are racing to the "forward" vans and the "defense/goalies" vans to get the best seat.

The two coaches got everyone in, we shut the doors, and I learned REALLY quickly that my ex-NHL coaches used to have people do everything for them when they were in the pros. They rose through a different type of youth hockey in their homelands, Lukas had spent some time playing professionally in Sweden but for the most part, it boiled down to this. I had to spoon feed them what was next, so I loved the autonomy I had from the start.

I texted the address of the hotel, and noticed them make brief eye contact – GAME ON. The two men sprinted to their vans with their group of players to see which one could get their first. Pavel played '80s music in his van but Lukas turned off the radio. Then they took off. Meanwhile, I realized I better just "be the van" and trust the fact that I can do anything. I signed up for this and was perfectly capable of keeping up with these mothafuckas.

I started to drive, but never quite figured out how to stop the air vents blowing freezing cold air directly at my face, full blast. That was for the best, though, because that was the only thing saving me from the horrible stench surrounding my breathing space. It reminded me of the smell of the monkey house from the zoo. Clearly, the last driver of this cargo van must have left me a secret message to spare me from the putrid odor of 18 hockey bags.

The stench of hockey boy sweat is no joke. I could taste it. My hair smelled like it. My clothes absorbed the various odors of different diets, gloves filled with months of sweat, boogers, and warts, the stench of pubescent ass mixed with a hint of Downey from the one mom who sanitized everything and ensured that anything touching skin had been freshened up to the scent of fresh cotton linen. God bless her.

As I mouth-breathed, I affectionately named the smell "Schwoitz" and decided to treat it as my passenger. Schwoitz was my Wilson, like the volleyball Tom Hanks relied on for companionship in the movie Castaway.

Then I realized I was driving in Boston. Holy shit, it had been awhile since I drove with aggressive lane changes and exit signs that came out of nowhere. I could faintly make out the coaches' vans which were about 4 cars ahead of me, so I trusted that as long as I could keep my GPS volume on loud and follow, I'd be okay. Of course, that was a horrible idea because, at some point, the coaches cut over two lanes and exited the turnpike. My GPS was in the circle of search death, still telling me to do a U-turn from when I left the terminal. I may or may not have just closed my eyes and swerved to make the exit; let's just say I was lucky I didn't cause an accident under the Ted Williams tunnel and end up on the next day's news: "Colorado woman driving a cargo van full of hockey equipment found dead on the Massachusset's turnpike. Her last words were... SCHWOITZ! Where are you? SCHWOITZ, I'm sorry!!!!"

Aside from a cracked tooth, I arrived at our hotel in Andover in one piece. I soon realized I belonged in hockey when I could chirp Lukas for saying "underwear" every time he tried to pronounce Andover.

As the boys retrieved their bags, their excitement was electric. No parents, just a giant sleepover with their best buddies. We passed out their room keys and instructed the boys to meet back in the lobby in 15 minutes.

The nice thing about being the only woman on the trip is that I had my own room. I quickly dropped off my stuff, used the bathroom for the first time since getting off the plane and checked my pants for shit stains from the harrowing ride. After a quick spritz of body spray to cover up the Schwoitz, I headed to the lobby to meet up with the group.

We all piled back into the passenger vans, me riding shotgun with a coach, and on to an Italian restaurant to carb-load we went. Rookie mistake, I let the kids order off the menu. It is much better to order spaghetti and meatballs and chicken parmesan for 25 people. Eighteen boys, two coaches and myself equals 25 because you'll have a couple of kids who can eat their body weight in spaghetti.

You quickly learn, however, that YOU YOURSELF cannot eat like a hockey player. Carb-loading on these weekends will add weight to that bootylicious physique you attempt to squeeze into your mom stretchy jeans, and unless you want to live in black leggings the rest of your days, start eating those salads and choosing your own food off the menu. Same goes for the hockey dads who volunteer, you can't wear black stretchy pants unless you want your kid to stop playing hockey. Forever.

I have to say, these kids were well-adapted to restaurant eating. They did teach me "shoe-checking" (a contest on who can put sauce or dressing on a teammate without getting caught, said checked teammate has to sing a song to the restaurant by standing on their chair). They seemed to politely ask waitstaff for more water or bread, they used napkins and utensils, and shockingly did not empty the salt shakers or throw food. There was an occasional spit ball from a straw, but for the most part, this team was still trying to impress their NHL coach staff and probably had a mom-threat that they would be killed at home if they caused any problems.

After the boys had been fed, I had one of two things to worry about. Here's a tip for team managers: try to get everything ordered from Sam's Club or know what you want from Costco, because you have to get all the Gatorades, water, bars, fruit and snacks lined up for the week. Peanut M&Ms, Cliff Bars, chocolate milk and bananas are staple hockey fuel although you'll find out that Entemenn's Little Bites and Welch's Fruit Snacks create an underground smuggling ring amongst the boys. Men and their food.

Another thing you'll quickly realize is that if your son has older brothers, he has an advantage, because hoarding and concealing the evidence is rule #1. I felt bad for the kids who were the only child or had just a sister because it was rough for them. They found themselves without Little Bites unless they ate them all at once. Their "trust" that teammates will share goes right out the window when the Lord of the Flies mentality takes over. I knew that this was a rite of passage for some, so I stayed back knowing that, as the warden, my job was just to keep the peace and let the natural mobsters run the joint.

Do not underestimate the fact that the parents who are there need to step up. It is A LOT of physical labor to buy all the drinks, snacks and food on a Costco run. However, getting this out of the way on day one is critical and, based on your schedule, you'll find that many parents arrive the following day so this becomes your job. Keeping receipts, loading and unloading the van, grabbing the valet cart at the hotel and drafting a few boys to have you put it all in your room takes a few hours, so plan accordingly. If you can find a willing parent to do the run for you and pre-pay with the team card, you are in good hands. Otherwise, embrace the suck and get it done.

Bedtime routines are trickier. Coach didn't pick captains that year, so he took the role of collecting all the phones in an empty pillowcase and telling each room that lights-out was 10:00 p.m. and to meet for breakfast by 8 a.m. I would then ask the front desk to set up wakeup calls for each room for 7:30 a.m. At U14, about half our parents still traveled, and many of them stayed at the hotel and hid in the wings. Like teenagers slipping out at night, they slowly made their way to the hotel lobby for a few drinks to proudly salute themselves for raising a son that could walk and talk on their own.

The kids soon learn that there are some things they have to learn when mom or dad isn't in the same hotel room. The boys have to learn to poop when their roommate is 5 feet away with their cell phone ready to record any incriminating bodily sounds. They need to learn how to air out their own equipment, hang their jerseys, and keep their used underwear and socks away from the clean stuff (yeah right).

Note to parents: at this age just accept the fact that they will put everything wet in the same overnight bag as the dry stuff. Their toothbrush is laying on the bathroom counter right next to their roommate's inhaler, and the petri dish of intermingled germs and DNA-migration is inevitable. They don't even *unwrap* the little soap. My guess is that if one were to scope a crime scene of a hockey team, everyone's DNA would be on everything the team touched. The "who-dun-it" would be impossible to flesh out unless you had video of the crime, and even then, they look so much alike at this age that a wrongful conviction would result in a mistrial based on reasonable doubt.

As I bundled up for a chilly Massachusetts morning, I sprayed my scarf with body spray and wound it around my neck the way I used to walk in Chicago to work in the winters. I turned on the ignition, only to feel the burst of icy, dusty air blowing directly in my face. I reacted by putting the scarf over my nose to protect this assault on my senses, only to discover the utilitarian nature of a scented scarf. The "Fart Scarf" was treating my PTSD from the olfactory assault of the hockey bags once again united in the back of my van. Schwoitz was definitely in the van with me, such a good companion.

Still trying to figure out if this van had any temperature controls, I started to notice the defroster wasn't working but, as expected, the coaches were racing off, only to stop at the hotel entrance because I had not provided them with the address to the rink! Haha mothafuckas, where do you think you are going so fast? As they stuck their heads out the window, in comes the text from my son..."where r we goin?" *Mwahahahah, your souls are mine!*

My foggy windows allowed me a nice 8x11 inch space to see the road, so I texted the address, and off to the games we went. Once we unloaded and found out what locker room we were in, I pulled out the roster stickers for the game sheets, crossing out the injured, and had about 60 minutes to catch my breath. I had forgotten my coffee at the hotel, but that was probably just as well, as I was completely over-caffeinated at this point. I opted for a warm bottle of Gatorade from the team supply, and immediately realized two things: 1) the taste of Blue Ice is really disgusting, and 2) all that time I spent whitening my teeth with Crest Whitening Strips was a waste of money. I just drank a full cup of blue sugar.

Game, win or loss, the boys at this age are just as happy and excited regardless of the outcome to get back on the bus. At this phase of hockey, it is FUN. The teams at this level are all pretty motivated to play in the NHL. They truly believe that anything is possible if you work hard. Nobody in their lives tells them they "can't" because nobody really knows that they can't. They are still growing, developing their hockey skills and they have no idea how to talk to girls. You have a few that have "girlfriends" (usually meaning girls they cyber-stalk), but everything is about hockey and Xbox. At this age, they are carefree except for the kid whose parents divorced (always give that kid extra snacks).

Think about it, they get to fly on a plane together, eat at restaurants, play an awesome sport they love, stay at hotels, pile into each other's rooms to watch movies and shoot the shit, eat fruit snacks and goldfish, and call their parents once or twice that weekend. Homework? Ha! Except for a few who have the threat of death at home, most boys in 8th grade or freshman year can still manage missing Fridays and make it up without affecting their grades. As parents, though, it is your job to ensure your kid understands that freshman year grades WILL affect their hockey or academic future, so be involved. I watched a couple of kids tank their grades their freshman year. Fortunately there is the Western Hockey League that pre-pays for college if they decide to go that route.

Looking back at this trip, I couldn't tell you who we played, how we did, or how many points my kid had. Some dad was keeping stats for those, I should see if he still has them. What I can tell you is that these boys probably had no idea how lucky they truly were to have these opportunities.

Parents, your money is well spent at this age because what hockey teaches them are coping skills, teamwork, and how to function in society as a well-adjusted person. There are some spoiled brats that come through the ranks, but our team seemed to counteract that with a few chirps to shut it down. Each kid finds their role both on and off the ice, whether it's Locker Boxing champion, best impersonator, funniest one-liner guy, Mr. Sensible, Mr. Dumb-ass, or the kid who actually folds his clothes in the locker room. They find their niche and that persona follows them through their teen playing years unless they move on to another team. It's fun to watch, they all just want to be connected to something bigger than themselves. Self-esteem, friendship, camaraderie – all from playing a sport where everyone is truly connected to a common goal. What they experience is unity through group-think in some ways, but can be themselves individually as well. Regardless of which side of politics their parents are on, the boys at this age are about immediate gratification from the rush of playing an intense sport.

The dichotomy of a hockey player is that they can seem like a doofus until they set foot on the ice. Think about it, if you play hockey, you must learn how to balance on two sharp pieces of metal while skating full speed holding a stick, sometimes backwards and sideways...keeping a small piece of rubber away from an opponent without getting crushed by bodies coming directly at you who are also trying to prevent you from shooting said rubber into a few open spaces in a 72x48 inch net.....protected by a guy dressed up like Optimus Prime.... whose only job is to shut down all of your efforts because his entire existence is to become an octopus with 8 brains who can read your every move. Pretty impressive. I marveled at the athleticism and coordination these boys had at the age of 14. Over the coming seasons, it got faster and even more skilled but at this age, they were all diamonds in the rough.

On the last day of the tournament, we had a night game. After dropping the boys off, I parked the car in an open spot between two other cars. I would later realize that you should never park a cargo van in a regular parking spot.

After the game, people are coming and going out of the parking lot, as a new game is bringing in a new stream of spectators and players. After checking both side mirrors, I began inching my way out of my space, only to notice headlights pointing directly at my driver's side waiting for me to "move it" so they could get through the parking lot to find a spot. So I inched back a bit more, felt a light "crunch-tap" sound, moved forward, and completed my 8-point turn to get out and find the locker room exit for the boys to load up. That's when Crazy New York Hockey mom came at me like Glenn Close at the end of Fatal Attraction. Even her frizzy blonde hair seemed to be on the warpath, Medusa-like.

She screamed in her thick New York accent, "Did you just fuckin' hit my car you fuckin' bitch? Yeah, you did, you hit my fuckin' car you fuckin' bitch. I just got that car and you hit my fuckin' car, what the hell you fuckin' asshole bitch?"

Ah, that was the crunch-tap I recalled from my 8-point turn. Rather than meet her anger with a guilty response, I looked at her with a calm, if puzzled expression and said, "Who, me?"

Wrong tactic. She cranked up the volume on her voice, repeating the same "you hit my brand new fuckin' car when you backed up, I saw you, don't you dare act all innocent you fuckin' asshole bitch," dropping another 7 or so f-bombs before I could even respond.

At this point, a few parents off in the distance noticed I was involved in some kind of altercation but nobody acted on it, maybe they assumed I knew the crazy lady or just stayed safe in their little circle away from my "job" as team manager. I walked away from the wimpy bystanders and went over to her car to assess the damage. To my chagrin, I saw 3-4 small white lines on her 2018 brand new Nissan

Armada whose ass was sticking out 4 extra feet from her parking spot directly backing to my spot. I know for a FACT that car was not there when I parked, so I would like to point out for the record, any self-respecting new car owner should park their car *far* away from any white cargo vans that need to back out. Preferably directly under street lights. We then walked over to the van to see if the marks lined up with anything on my van. I did not see a single scratch or remnant but decided that purchasing the liability insurance for the van WAS a good idea and patted my psyche on the back knowing that this episode was about to turn into a Law and Order crime scene if it didn't calm down. At this point, both Lukas and Pavel walked over.

Picture big hockey guys with thick European accents on either side of me asking what was going on. At that point, I thought she would shut her trap, take a dip in the clue bag that I had protection from two big muscular guys with accents that sounded like Drago. I felt like a Boss in that moment: a little bit Queen Latifah, a little bit Uma Thurman from Kill Bill. Their presence seemed to affect her use of the f-bomb, but not her crazy. I heard one of them mutter under their breath that they thought she was drunk, which didn't help much.

That's when I piped in, saying we should take pictures and deal with this calmly. No response. Then I remembered how I felt when anyone tells me to calm down. Not good. That's when I told her I was a lawyer, and if she wanted to go to court, I'd be happy to take this on as I was the one who was feeling threatened at this point.

Wrong move. She unleashed again, starting from the top of her earlier monologue, sprinkling in some new, even less flattering superlatives to make her commentary even more colorful.

At that point, another dad, who owned his own body shop in Colorado, took a look at the "damage" and explained to her that it could be buffed and fixed for about $300. This induced a calm between her rage-fit storms, and we were finally able to take pictures, exchange licenses, etc.

The irony of the situation was that her son's team had just been annihilated in their game, and this Mama Bitch was unloading her unholy rage in a crime of passion. The nice thing about the New York Hockey mom was that, in the coming days, we settled everything in a few texts. Insurance was going to cover it all, and her final sign-off was "have a great season" with a smiley face emoji. It was our grown-up version of the ceremonial glove pump the boys do after a game.

Surreal as that entire experience was, new versions of it played out in future games as the competition got more intense. What happens to the hockey parent brain when watching your player play? Aside from being a spectator, there seems to be a feeling that you are also on the ice with your player as your Avatar. Something to do with mirror neurons, only amplified because it is your kid getting smashed by someone you don't know. I've witnessed moms with sympathy pains scream at the kid who did it as if he were Satan on ice, then heard a loud dad respond, "Shut up and let them play." I often wonder what these moms are hoping to accomplish. Some type of repentance, maybe in the form of his chastened parents going down to the ice and spanking their son on the ass? Perhaps grabbing the announcer's mike and apologizing to the stands for his awful hockey behavior called..... checking?

If your team loses, and God help you if you are the parent to the goalie who let in a muffin, your body releases cortisol and now you are under stress. Too bad there's no way to snort serotonin before games: we'd all be less angry and depressed. I knew a fellow team manager dad who experienced a heart attack after a game; so much anxiety and increased heart rate during his son's game that he actually ended up in the ER. No thanks, hit the fitness room at the hotel before the games, get all that pent up shit out of your system, dawg!

I remember feeling like shit after a tournament game, just depleted from being a full-time servant to the kids and coaches. I was done. I went into the hotel lobby and sat on a super-stuffed-fluffy leather couch. It beckoned me like a hot Krispy Kreme glazed donut on a cold winter day. I needed to sit for a second and think about something other than hockey. I had given up on trying to convince myself that my new winter boots were actually comfortable and warm, so I took them off to rub my feet. My face was so haggard, my cell phone face recognition stopped working.

The lobby of the hotel was filled with regular customers. It was a larger, more expensive hotel this time. I never understood how we did not have more control over where we stayed for some of our tournaments. Oftentimes we were given a list of options from the tournament director to our hockey organization who had a middle man. The list did not always make it to the team manager (me) in a timely manner. Much like ticket scalpers, some hockey team managers are pros at snagging the cheapest hotel that is closest to the rink. They also have friends in town that give them the low-down so having the jump start is inevitable. In Colorado, we were usually the outsiders. We got the most expensive and furthest from the rink option.

From my standpoint, I was happy to have the luxurious Krispy Kreme donut couch for my tired soul. As I started to put my boots back on, a very handsome man approached me. He was dressed for business, perhaps coming off of a meeting with clients at the nearby Ruth Chris Steakhouse. He was tall, had dark wavy hair and a beautiful smile. With his Latin accent, he said "Excuse me miss, would you like some coffee?" I was taken aback, not in any condition to be noticed by Rico Suave. For one moment, I felt like a human being and not a frazzled troll doll from the '80s. Then I realized he was looking at my chest. I was still trying to decide whether to be offended or flattered when it occurred to me that I was wearing a sweatshirt that said "Needs More Caffeine." One of my friends on the team bought it for me as they understood I was only able to function with strong coffee on these trips. I liked my coffee so strong it needed to show up on a drug test. I looked down at my shirt, made a pig-snort sound, looked up again and said "You mean my shirt? I'm Hil-AR-IOUS" in a way-too-loud voice. I proceeded to awkwardly pause, then had a massive laugh attack like a psycho. That's when I realized I could have used a stiff drink and a real donut. And that hockey did not rule my life, I was still a real person. Slightly deranged, though? Probably...

There were times when I'd feel great about what I was doing for the team, knowing that the coaches were spending a lot of time developing these kids to make it to the top of the rankings. I picked up a few tricks to make my post-tournament week more manageable. I had asked the coaches to let me use the team credit card for every expense. They were so easy to work with and appreciated my help, they did whatever I asked if it made them less accountable for administrative bullshit. It was easier for me to keep all the receipts and reconcile online statements. When I got home, I'd submit everything so the organization could divide up the travel costs and the parents could have the total they needed to pay as fast as possible. Being asked to pay two tournament fees in the same month was financially insane for most of us. Our hockey bills felt like an insurance deductible for a roof replacement.

We had mastered the van rentals as a primary form of transportation for the team and equipment. It had worked well financially, plus we liked being independent. Sometimes relying on a bus driver was a drag, they always wanted advanced itineraries and expected big tips. We liked the freedom that our wild west attitude allowed, plus we were cheap and the parents were behind any way we could shave off a few hundred bucks for each tournament.

On our way back from a tournament at the University of Notre Dame, we took the Indiana tollway into the southside of Chicago. I had been raised in the south suburbs of Chicago, so getting to Midway was easy and I was proud of my old stomping grounds. I had street smarts and knew where to go for the best Italian beef, the cheapest gas, and how to navigate the highway system. If you're not from there and someone says "take the Dan Ryan" they don't tell you that it is both I-90 (aka Kennedy expressway and Chicago Skyway and Jane Addams Memorial) and I-94 (Kingery Expressway, Bishop Ford, also the Kennedy, Edens expressway and eventually the Tri-state). It all depends on what part of the highway you are on to distinguish which "name" to use. It gets very confusing. And then you hear "go east toward the Lake" which also means nothing if you are from Colorado where you can actually see the mountains as landmarks. The Lake is nowhere in sight until you are on Lake Shore Drive and if you are there, you are nowhere near the airport. Listening to a Chicagoan tell you how to get somewhere, you'll get a history lesson on naming conventions that mean nothing to your GPS. So I was proud to be the token Chicagoan. After a stop at Portillo's for some beef "samwiches" and chocolate cake, a few hamburgers for the kids who didn't trust the hot giardiniera, I advised the crew that we needed to stay together and to not stop.

We had three vans. In front of the caravan, Grapes was driving. He was the assistant coach that weekend and was excited to drive the defensemen and the goalies. Grapes never had cash, he was a former D3 collegiate hockey player that was still living the hockey dream. He liked the free travel and modest perks of coaching youth hockey. He also played twice a week in the beer league and wasn't ready to fully adult yet. He was fun to have around, had some great chirps and stories from his glory days. He loved his mother, talked about how much he and his brother would fist fight as kids and had some other interesting viewpoints on life. He encouraged the players to do well in school cautioning them how he regretted not focusing more on his GPA. It had something to do with limiting his college hockey opportunities.

I had the monkey-house-fart-funk-cargo van with all the equipment, Schwoitz was still my only passenger. The head coach was driving the forwards and his wife was in the passenger seat.

We had to stop for gas and were pressed for time, so I sent a text to all the drivers of the vans, warning that we should not stop until we got closer to the airport because "what you hear about crime in Chicago" is true. I was not afraid of getting shot, just carjacked - I was a single woman in a cargo van and I wasn't packing heat to defend myself. The Coloradans were only familiar with mass shootings by white teenage males, this was an entirely different landscape. Too much for a simple hockey parenting book, but I'd been in some tight spots in my own teenage years and managed to escape unscathed.

As we started to slow down for the tolls, I heard a light tap on my passenger side window. I thought, "*aw shit, here we go...what do I have on me?*" My purse was underneath the seat and my phone was in my hand, not much to work with. I was in between both vans full of kids. Before I panicked, I caught the sight of the coach's wife's hair blowing in the wind. There she was, standing in the middle of a tollway lane tapping on my window. Phew, it was not a carjacking but rather ....what DA-FUQ is she doing? I told them all not to stop or get out for any reason except......

I rolled down the window and she blurted out - WE NEED THE CARD. The team card!!!!

Okay... alright. I loved how they respected the vision of keeping all the expenses on the card, but I was not prepared for the relay of a credit card on a major highway in an area that was not exactly the place to get out of your car. So I dug my purse from under the seat (never leave your purse on a seat, it's like chum for a shark). Fishing out the credit card, I leaned across to give it to her and watched her run to the van in front of me to give it to Grapes. Meanwhile, in true Chicago fashion, a series of honking horns and foul-mouthed expletives were being hurled by what felt like a thousand Mike Ditkas. Nobody gives a shit why we were stopped but seemed mad enough to shoot us over it if we didn't keep things moving. Waking up my south side version of situational awareness, everyone's bumpers were dented and damaged (suck it N.Y. mom!), so these folks would have nothing to lose by gently nudging our bumpers to drop the right hint. I was expecting it.

I watched this sweet woman in high heeled boots run to the driver side to hand Grapes the card. Then I watched her struggle with the passenger door. Oh yeah, I do remember someone saying that door was broken....we better let the rental agency know that's how we got it. Then I could see hockey players standing and shoving forward through their back window until finally somebody was able to open the side door. Next thing I see is her feet hanging horizontally out of the side door as if she were paddling to shore and then what looked like body surfing through the van as Grapes continued to drive forward. This grown woman had emigrated from a country in Europe, learned an entirely different language, birthed two kids and almost died on a Chicago tollway in a valiant attempt to keep the credit card system in place. At some point, I saw her head pop up in the back seat, she turned around with a wild-eyed smile and gave me the thumbs up. As I rolled forward into the tollway, the attendant was shaking his head at me and handed me the card saying, "Where in the hell are you all from, that's some stupid ass shit you just did." He had been instructed to charge all three tolls for our vans on the card and hand it back to me. I calmly replied, "We're a hockey team from Colorado and want to put all the tolls on this card please... thank you" and went on to the airport, trying not to pee my pants from laughing so hard. I didn't want to admit I was from Chicago, much easier to adopt the stereotypical pot smoking Colorado hippie in that moment.

I had learned how to pick my battles on what stories or situations left the group. As a team manager, you become the handler. Think Harvey Keitel as the Cleaner from Pulp Fiction. Aside from a few things, the kids were pretty good at hotels because I told them I had eyes everywhere, which was true. I later learned that the 16U team in the organization had thrown mac and cheese on the ceiling, cracked a toilet, broken a mirror, and used Tinder to hook up with local girls. Not my circus, not my monkeys. But I did use it as a teachable moment, telling our boys that they need to think about the minimum wage worker who has to clean the ceiling and repair the toilets. Good 'ole fashioned Catholic guilt, works every time. Also mentioned that underage Tinder hookups at hotels are illegal and they'll end up with a painful pee-pee disease or maybe be killed by a 42 year old serial killer. No mincing words, the boys insisted that they did not participate in any of those shenanigans. Yeah right, I could make any one of them crack under pressure. But at the end of the day, nobody got hurt. Nothing spelled relief like Sunday night in my own bed, though I did look like a troll doll from the '80s on Monday morning. And my cell phone's face recognition never worked again.

10

THE SCOUTIES AND THE SHOW

E nter: the men in black.

Not coaches, not dads... but scouts who show up to watch tournaments as soon as things get more competitive. Certain teams or players will draw them in based on a tip from a coach or scout who had a summer gig to check out a few rising stars. Coaches who know other coaches start piecing together teams with the hope of making some quick cash and developing the tournament as one of the "elites" by invitation only. My son had a good amount of these, but looking back there was one truly valuable experience because it had been organized by a USHL team's General Manager. Great experience. At the Bantam level, there are a lot of opportunities for kids, but don't get upset if your kid got bypassed, plenty more where that came from!

Navigation Tip: Don't get wrapped up in FOMO if your player didn't get an invite. Sometimes these things are predetermined by dad coaches who happen to have connections to rinks and tournament organizers. It's a way to make money, not a pre-destined ticket to the NHL.

~

At the ripe old age of 14, the Western Hockey League (WHL) sends scouts to watch the players. That draft is at the end of the season. Then there is the USA Hockey National Team Development Program (NTDP) that starts a short list and eventually produces NHL draft picks and top college commits. Things change as to which league or program or state sends the most people to the juniors, to NCAA programs and/or the NHL. There are companies that send scout-looking-dudes who are evaluating and writing "Scouting Reports" which, if you're gullible enough, you'll pay money to read beyond the 1-2 sentence blurb they provide in the email. I did it twice, which made me stress out even more as I compared notes to all the other players on his team. What they wrote about my son was great! But then they rate them against each other, giving them grades and already identifying who is draftable. For the purposes of this book I went back and looked at all the comments from our team. They got it half right; the other half was way off.

Now keep in mind, there are dozens of junior hockey leagues and hundreds of junior hockey teams in the Hockey Universe. There are different paths to D1 if that's where the kid wants to eventually end up, but plenty of online resources explain how to assess it. This chapter is about the scouts.

The scouts definitely have a certain look. Typically, they are younger men ranging in age from 25-40. Nice haircuts, some with a wavy-flow-Patrick Dempsey look a la Grays Anatomy, and some with a shorter cut much like a Great Clips poster. They're usually wearing nice dress shoes with expensive athletic fit jeans or sporty looking golf pants, probably Lululemon. They never wear hats, and their jackets are straight out of the CCM or Bauer catalog or maybe they want to be more incognito and go with a black puffy jacket from North Face or Patagonia.

A few of them have a single pen and a black, leather-bound manual. Others have computers or iPads. There are a few older guys with baggy jeans and non-descript jackets straight out of the '90s.

They don't give a shit what they look like, but they definitely have messier notebooks, wear readers, and study the line charts in plain view while scribbling their comments.

Look to the outskirts of the rink: some are congregating. You never know who they are there to watch as they slink in and out of games like spies. They sometimes watch the game from the highest point of the rink if there is a cafe table and chairs. Or they live on the side of the rink, closer to the team bench. Occasionally you'll see them talking to a hockey advisor or a coach after the game, but for the most part they have some type of mysterious personality that is calculating stats, marking things off of checklists and maybe recording a quick snippet of a play on their phone to confirm their understanding that the kid (or team) they came to watch was worth writing about.

As a parent, you're hoping they're noticing how *awesome* your player is. Most of the time if your kid does something amazing, the guy's looking down, or just left the rink. Or your kid shits the bed, and that's what they saw. How they play the game is what they're assessing, hockey IQ, skating, physicality and a few other things once they watch more games. As a hockey team manager, you're curious if they got the line charts or scouting sheets that you've spent hours creating and getting printed in time for the tournament.

Throughout the year, you may recognize the same scout, but for the most part you start to realize that it doesn't matter what you know or think you know. They have an agenda, and you are not a part of it, so stay out of the way and smile if they make eye contact. They may be looking at dad to see if he is tall. Occasionally you'll see a CCM-jacket wearing dad with Skechers walk over, maybe he knows the scout or had another hockey player in the family. You never know who is who; that scout could eventually get a job as a coach in the USHL. It's a small world. All you can do is cross your fingers and hope that any notes made about your kid are good ones.

If you are approached, it is important to not look too excited or desperate. The first time a scout asked if I was the mother, I immediately became self-conscious of a dry-bat-in-the-cave booger in my nostril that was flapping as I was breathing. As I rubbed my nose, he'd rub his nose and that went on and on until I realized that I was supposed to be answering questions as innocuously as possible. The key here is to play it cool, keep your cards close to your chest. No need to say, "Oh no that's okay, my son wants to play in the USHL and go to college to play hockey. Probably not interested in the WHL, but thanks!" Don't say that.

Whether it's a scout or a potential advisor, your player is being assessed on many different levels. It's not always how many points they have, but it certainly doesn't hurt. They watch his body language on the bench. On the ice. Leaving the locker room. If the kid ignores his parents and walks straight to their friends or girlfriend, that's minus a point. If they are being loud or disrespectful, minus a point. If they are ordering fries and Coke at the cafe rather than drinking their water with electrolytes, that can also show signs of being undisciplined on diet. Being considerate, like holding the door open or being cognizant of where they throw their bag as they circle up to a group. They are judging character, they are judging parents, and they are judging overall sportsmanlike behavior of the family unit. Think about it, if you have two 6'0 feet tall defensemen, relatively similar skills and GPA, they are going to take the kid that knows how to behave in public, as they don't want any trouble on their teams. Or the kid whose parents seem relatively normal. Knowledge is power and this stuff is drilled into your brain eventually, but nobody told me any of this when my kid was 14.

Navigation tip (for players): All eyes on character. Don't wear a baseball cap at tournaments, don't buy candy or Coke, hug your mother first (not your girlfriend), watch your mouth, shake hands and make eye contact with any adult that introduces themselves to you, support your team, watch your body language, don't post anything on social media, don't argue with the refs, don't start fights unless you have to defend your goalie, always have good sportsmanlike conduct. Listen to hockey podcasts, some of them really know what they're talking about.

~

By the second or third tournament of the season, the players become more aware of who may be watching. The coaches will talk to scouts about the players and introduce the player to them after the game.

As players depart from the bus, they mimic acting like men and not boys who play hockey. On their heads, they wear beanies with their Beats pushed up high on their temples, or air pods while walking with a stoic look. I chuckled as I watched them pass me with messily tucked dress shirts and crooked ties, maybe a team jacket uncharacteristically zipped up all the way to the top for the kid who didn't know how to tie the tie. I would wish them good luck and for one millisecond I could tell that they wished their own mom or dad were there telling them that. Maybe I project, but I would notice a glimmer of "I miss home" as they stepped off the bus.

When away from the scouties, the boys will boast about who is going to "The Show" as they recount game highlights for one another. Things like "having good character" by holding the door open and not shouting profanities outside the locker room or bus become part of the conversation at home.

By the time they're 14 and 15, kids are starting to get more looks and some kids are approached by agents and/or advisors who may be looking to add a prospect to their list. As of writing this book, there are rules governing contracts between a youth hockey player and an agent who works for an agency that handles NHL contracts. No money can change hands.

More common is the presence of the family advisor, or hockey advisor. Some are really good. Some are like vultures, circling around the kids like a personal trainer at a big gym. They've watched your player all season and see something that maybe the coach doesn't utilize. They are complimentary, they have some tips, and they can easily convince you that they're the guide you need on the path toward D1 and maybe the NHL. They may have a portfolio of the kids that made it. Advisors work for you. They have connections and maybe a really nice haircut and fancy watch. They are there for your kid, they will sherpa his ass through the entire process. They're not wearing flip-flops like you, they've got the right shoes.

There are fees associated with the hockey advisor, but they can help your player in many ways.

THE PROS:

- The player feels like they have someone who is "on their side" who is not a coach or a parent.
- The advisor has connections with coaches in the junior leagues or prep schools and can advise which path may be best for your player when it comes to teams, specialty camps, or college interest.
- The advisor has connections with scouts and can drum up conversations at the bar, in the hotel lobby or at the airport. They get to know the people who are writing the reports and ultimately they start marketing your kid's "brand."
- The advisor can help with tryouts at main camps, prospect camps and even new teams.
- Some advisors speak the truth, even telling families what they really need to hear, even if it means playing in a different league with a longer path to the promised land.

THE CONS:

- Some advisors don't yet have the connections, but they're hoping to!
- Some have too many players and can't provide personal attention, especially if your player is not their top prospect.
- Prices vary; some have a fixed price that expires once the

player is drafted to the team they want. Anywhere between
$2,000-$3,500, could be more.
- Some have yearly prices that get renewed until either
party dissolves the contract. Read the fine print.
- Some advisors are not worth it at all.

One way to avoid the headache is to vet the advisors. Ask for the
phone numbers of parents who are currently contracted because,
again, there is no YELP review for these people. They have fancy
websites, business cards and success stories with testimonials, but it's
best to do your own research. It needs to be a good fit, and your kid is
the product. I've known players who never got one until they were
already in the juniors. They saved themselves a few thousand bucks!
Some players have been through 2 or 3, with families shelling out
$2500 a pop. Buyer beware, no guarantees and definitely not required
in the early years.

Whether your player makes it to "The Show" or gets on the prep
school team, you may have to rely on the advice of other sherpas
more than not. It's a dog-eat-dog world out there, people start to get
nervous when players and advisors are huddled in the corners after
big tournament games. You'll watch an advisor, the player, and a
parent talking to another hockey-looking-guy and you'll find yourself
scouring their jackets looking for any insignia of who they may be
with. It's mind-numbing how insecure we all get and absolutely
infuriating when you spend money and realize you just funded that
guy's golf vacation in Arizona. Aw hell, this sherpa definitely made a
few mistakes. Still amateur hour.

When my son was 15, he was invited to the USA Hockey National
Player Development Camp. Players earn their spot through their
performance at a series of state and district level games held after
their regular hockey season. It felt like a big deal, a few of his
teammates also made it and the games that summer were very
competitive. I was told that this holy grail of camps was one of the
ways to identify the "top talent," and that if he was lucky enough to
shine, it was a springboard for future opportunities. This experience

is a snapshot in time. A close up and humbling view of the cream of the crop. I've seen quite a few of those names in the World Juniors and drafted into the NHL.

Talent comes in many forms. Skilled, fast and big with high hockey IQ are the obvious threats. The next level are the players with flashes of greatness, things like scoring aptitude, competitiveness, and anything that allows them to stand out. Every last bit of grit has to be brought to the table with grace and good sportsmanship. If your kid takes a shit on his mental strength, he's done. Flashy won't matter but a little cocky is okay, as long as his character is in check. There are some kids there with a reputation that precedes them, but it is vital that your kid does not let that get to him.

Again, so many variables can affect an outcome and confidence is a huge factor. All I know is that the rink that week was crawling with scouts, so many CCM and Bauer jackets that someone could film a new series called Hockey Scout Clone Wars. Easy to spot the nervous parents in small groups looking like they wanted to crawl straight up the ass of hockey to assure the powers that be that their kid was *THE* kid to watch. The stress that week caused night sweats and jaw pain. If I could go back, I wouldn't have gone to watch because there was nothing I could actually do except pray. For the kids on the team that didn't make the camp, they still FOUGHT their way up to the next league. Some did not continue playing, some are still living the dream. This national camp is a great way to be found, but not the only way. Again, the kid has to prove themselves over and over and over again against the odds unless they are the 1% of all youth players. The odds of making it are no joke.

Navigation Tip: Trust your gut before hiring a family advisor. Shop around, don't get into bed on the first date, wait if it's not right.

Finding the best developmental opportunity is really the key factor in deciding "what to do" and "where" to go next. It takes honest feedback and money. Prep schools in the Northeast have a separate ethos than in AAA travel clubs, this is where a good advisor can be worth his salt. If there is good coaching, objectivity and support (both financially and mentally) you are golden. If...if...if... You just don't know, so do your homework, make a list of pros and cons, listen to your kid and make sure they are mature enough to leave home before plunking down a fortune.

Oh yeah, and enjoy the game. You will miss watching them play someday, despite the alien of twisted stress that lives in your gut from this point on. For Pete's sake, make sure you aren't always talking about hockey to your normal friends, or you'll start to sound insane. When your non-hockey friend always wears the same shirt when they see you that says, "You're killin' me Smalls!" it's time to take the hint.

Your honor, I'd like to state the facts for the sake of Average Joes with no former hockey knowledge or ties. Here's my take on it:

Hockey is a three-lane highway, and the one all the way to the left is the Lexus lane. Otherwise known as the Express Lane. The cars in this lane are made up of hockey prodigies, some of them born to former players in the NHL. If said legacies have fathers that coach at this level, then your kid needs to be mindful in the locker room that bashing the coach is never a good idea. Remember, the coach is someone's father. And they talk about hockey at dinner. Those kids are good hockey players, they have good genetics, live-in video review, and their route is pre-scouted. Can't wish for another family, so stay in the middle lane sonny and hope you can play well enough to get on that kid's line. Just gotta work hard.

If you have an ex-NHL coach for your team, there is no doubt that they understand the rules of hockey. Nobody questions their love of the game, their knowledge of how to play it, or their aptitude for winning. Just like any other fan, they want to see their kid score or do something amazing. Whatever advantages those kids have, every athlete on their team needs to figure out how to work with their coach and the circumstances. I have to say, we sure love it when a famous athlete's kid does well in the same sport. Bobby and Brett

Hull, Gordie, Mark and Marty Howe, Peter Stastny and sons Yan and Paul, JP and Zach Parise are just a few hockey greats. Not to miss all the other famous families too: Archie, Peyton and Eli Manning, Bobby and Barry Bonds, Muhammad and Laila Ali, Dale Earnhardt Sr. and Jr., I'm sure there's more. I couldn't resist watching Tiger's teenage son Charlie tee up for the PNC golf championship together. So cute! Go Charlie!

The next is the middle lane. This is for the players that are big and skilled. Or Canadian. Or from Finland. Or any other snow-packed country or state. Or just really rich dads who own ice rinks or manage a junior hockey team. Now some kids under 5'10" still make it to the NCAA and/or the NHL. There are plenty of examples of the playmakers and snipers that prove to dominate this lane with something other than size. However, you'll attend the College Hockey seminar where they will avoid the topic and focus on skill, GPA and holier than thou character they are looking for, but then one of those coaches will blurt out "size," and the cat's out of the bag. Suddenly, the big kids look relieved while the shorties of the group take the first punch to the gut, realizing they may not get much taller than they are now, and it'll be sink or swim. Some parents get their kid's wrists X-rayed to see if their growth plates are still open and get the estimate on height early on. Brilliant. At one presentation before a camp, there was a Cornell hockey grad who had a phenomenal hockey career. He shared that his height was only 5'6", his words were "size doesn't matter unless you let it." Great advice if your kid can see it that way.

If you need a little booster for undersized stature, have your player listen to US Navy Admiral William H. McRaven's commencement speech that starts with making your bed as a good habit. He specifically talks about the "munchkin crew," none of whom were over 5'5", but all of whom were the fastest of their 7 boats. Despite being made fun of for the size of their flippers, they outperformed all the others and had the last laugh. Nothing mattered but their will to succeed.

It is by far one of the best motivational speeches I've ever heard, rivaled only by Eminem's "Lose Yourself" if you're pressed for time.

The right lane is for anyone who just isn't there yet. People refer to them as the late-bloomers or the ones who just don't have it, but refuse to give up playing. They have potential to develop and if they can keep up with middle lane traffic. They love hockey, no matter what. This group should definitely start reviewing the stats on how difficult it is to make it to the NCAA or the NHL for that matter, especially if the parents are writing checks without analyzing the situation. They'll get passed up, but some of them will merge into the middle lane. Plenty of stories of athletes who were grinders in the juniors who, against all odds, made it to "The Show." Mental resilience and passion for the game. It's about clawing your way and never giving up. As Arnold Palmer once said, "Golf is a game of inches. The most important are the six inches between your ears." There are hundreds of teams in a multitude of leagues, getting to play Division II or Division III hockey is a strong possibility. Just a different highway for some, perhaps an alternate off-road route.

Basically, if the kid isn't getting any looks by the time they're 21, maybe it's time to hang up the skates. Beer league is where everyone goes eventually. Despite my best attempt at singing like Janis Joplin at a Karaoke bar, I am not Janis Joplin, and never will be, despite my passion and fervent desire to sing like Janis Joplin. I did sing backup in a blues band a couple of times, I got a taste.

Check the stats, a good advisor will give you the lowdown. Remember, players from around the world are also trying to get into the same leagues, and their mindset is different, maybe it's cultural. By the time they make it here, they are elite. Develop, play with heart, and annihilate. No mystery there, just be realistic before spending another million dollars on the next level.

Now some parents are shelling out a few extra bucks for mental coaches, treating performance coaching much like a skating coach or personal trainer. A Phil Jackson for your budding Michael Jordan (God I wish he coached hockey!). Getting in THE ZONE. If your player is in a slump, doesn't have a good relationship with their coach, has a habit of replaying their mistakes in their head, or gives 100% effort without being productive there are some good performance coaches and books out there. We found a performance coach for one season; he was totally worth it. He had expert skills and I wish he lived close to us, I'd have him over for mid-life crisis counseling.

I had a scout tell me that his best players are a lot like a happy dog playing fetch with a tennis ball: they can play hockey all day every day. They never take their sights off the puck and they are ready to play. Hockey ready. Know anyone like that?

11

THE RUMSPRINGA

Balancing high school and a competitive sport with travel is extremely taxing on a kid, moreso if your player attends a traditional high school and needs to leave the state for big tournaments. And if the goal is to get into a NCAA Division 1 college to play hockey, the pressure is unyielding. Contrary to high school pre-internet, kids don't really have an excuse like the "library was closed" because Google never sleeps. Kids are expected to be 100% tech savvy, using laptops at the airport, submitting their homework assignments online while in their hotel room, communicating with teachers by email or between games, and basically operating their education like they have a job in a remote office. Here's a patchwork of perspectives that emerged amongst conversation with other hockey parents:

Hey kid, you're a talented hockey player. What are your grades?

- *Player perspective:* Let's see, to get into a D1 hockey school with all options available, I should be getting a 3.8 GPA so that I have a shot at more colleges (remember there is always someone bigger and better than you; your grades can give you the edge).

- *Player perspective:* I need to make sure I'm taking all my core classes. I also need to get into those Advanced Placement (AP) classes in case I go Ivy League and my parents win the lottery. I need to at least get a B in those (remember, there's always that guy on YouTube that can teach anything, praise the Lord for Khan Academy).
- *Player perspective:* Traveling this week for a tournament, we leave on Thursday and get back late Sunday night, 4 maybe 5 games to play. Don't forget to tell teachers that you're out for hockey (so, my teacher has 200 other students, I have to email him/her and talk to her/him too because he/she sometimes forgets. Friday is review day and Monday is the test, I'll have to get notes from somebody).
- *Player perspective:* Be a kid, go to Homecoming! (Nope, not if there's practice or a game).
- *Player perspective:* Play another sport (sure, when?).
- *Player perspective:* Don't forget, the best players practice all the time when they're not on the ice (get 500 shots in tonight after homework).
- *Player perspective:* Get enough sleep! (Except this weekend, we get home Sunday night at 11pm, assuming our equipment makes it. Study for the test on Monday at 8 a.m.)
- *Player perspective:* Eat your bodyweight in whole grains, protein, vegetables, fresh fruit, healthy fat and complex carbs (or whatever's available, smash some Timmy's if in Canada).
- *Player perspective:* Private lesson at 5 a.m. before school, should be enough time to shower and be in class by 8 a.m. The best players train all the time and get better by getting on the ice on the off-days (drink a protein drink after practice, better microwave a frozen burrito for the ride to school).
- *Player perspective:* Don't forget to stretch after dryland

workout, need to maintain flexibility (ignore the shoulder, that AC joint should be fine by now, work on stretching the hips. Tape the wrist. Be tough, everyone hurts).

I started to feel like Rocky's boxing coach, "C'mon kid...you gotta punch and punch until you can't punch no more." I also felt like a zoo-keeper, feeding the exotic animal copious amounts of meat. Perhaps an unpaid personal assistant who had to keep a schedule for a crowned prince. I'd occasionally enter a room like Igor, hunched over saying "Yes Master" to remind him that he better not turn into an entitled little prick. Needless to say, the kid was exhausted on most days of the week. It was astounding to me that he, and his teammates, were grinders at everything in their lives, not just hockey. It felt like too much and I'm an old-school "figure it out" kind of mom.

Some hockey parents admitted to lying to the school for their kids missing classes to avoid being considered truant. We all agreed that it was excessive, but just tried to keep the wheels moving to continue support for this system. Something about that collective spirit that keeps the families going.

Navigation Tip: There is a case to be made for moving closer to the rink or alternate methods of school (prep school, Study/Train/Play or hybrid/online school). If you drive more than one hour and the kid is carsick trying to do their homework in the car, just think how that extra 15 hours of study time will go to the kid in Minnesota or prep school who walks to the rink. There is also a case to be made that this level of pressure leads to burnout.

I decided to reach out to my son's high school counselor. She was like a member of the family who helped my two older sons cement their plans after graduation. She was worth her weight in gold, we were lucky to have her. I wanted her to know what he was doing and how to best create a DI-worthy schedule. My son and I met with her the summer after his freshman year. Looking back, this was extremely valuable as some kids didn't do this on his team and, as a consequence, struggled with time management and communication, thereby failing classes and tanking their GPA early on. She suggested taking one online class over the summer to lessen the load, perhaps a hybrid approach combining in-person with a few electives online. He decided that taking Spanish 4 was out of the question as the grade was primarily based on class participation. So much for mastering another language, we'll leave that up to the bilingual Swedish hockey players who come over to play in our leagues.

There were other classes that required group projects and deducted points for late submissions, all of which my son would have to figure out. Aside from hockey, joining other extracurricular clubs was limited; difficult to check another box besides hockey. At one point I jokingly suggested finding a mission trip to help a village in Africa get clean water. Turns out one of his teammates was planning on that. Seriously? Ok fine, then set up a prom dance for the senior center, work at the Humane Society or volunteer at the local food bank. All things the National Honor Society suggested in lieu of attending meetings. I started to wonder why we held such high standards for these teenagers, when I'm pretty sure a 16 year-old Swedish player will take his spot anyway. How are they SOOOO good?

Anyway, the good news is that when they reach the summit of the NCAA mountain, the hockey program is more conducive to the student athlete. Think about it, teachers must be in cahoots with the school so the student athlete is successful. Oh yeah, the prep schools care too, they want your money. Investing in you means banking on a solid income statement for the long haul. What a concept.

In general, hockey players are humble and these hard lessons often make them a good person, a better player, and maybe a fantastic coach someday. But this model? Does the CEO of Amazon work this hard?

The first two years of high school was a grueling experience, but he did well in both seasons and managed to maintain a good GPA. Oh yeah, and he only had minor injuries amongst a team with broken collarbones, dislocated AC joints, shoulder sprains and concussions. It is my recommendation that hockey players should focus their future education on physical therapy or becoming orthopedic surgeons given how many of them know how to rehab shoulder and hip issues. They already know what breaks and maybe how to fix it. Or maybe dentists.

It was time to think about a change in teams, as he'd been playing on the same line for two years in a row. As a 15 year-old, he'd been offered to play up at the 16U level but turned it down in order to stay "with the boys." I was proud of him for his loyalty (or fear of the unknown, not sure which). It was fun, but that could have helped him get drafted (looking back, if the athlete plays up their chances are greater to make the USHL draft but risk getting annihilated if they are not physically ready). He knew his role. He was a savvy playmaker, the kid had a great shot but was starting to plateau as the team had habits and not much was going to change.

So perhaps not a perfect analogy, but let's look at what the Amish do with the Rumspringa ritual. The Rumspringa is when the 16 year-old Amish teenager gets to venture out and "taste the modern world." The teens can leave the community, explore and experience forbidden fruits, all with an implicit understanding that if they decide to leave the community permanently, they will be shunned as a consequence. Here's what the Amish have over the hockey organizations: the Amish actually encourage their teens to LEAVE as part of the process.

Hockey's Rumspringa has a shroud of secrecy. I've heard it's called the mating season too. It behooves you as a family to avoid fanfare and quietly sneak out for peeks at prep schools or perhaps accept a skating invitation with another team so the coach can get a look at your player without compromising tryouts. It is challenging if the team dads or coaches start getting commitments by February though, so learning the art of not answering a question as a basis of becoming a politician someday may be a valuable skill, should they ever run for office. Be aware that in some organizations, a player may cross the path of a hockey Tony Soprano or risk getting blacklisted. Don't worry, if the player gets temporarily whacked (metaphorically speaking) and maintains integrity, they'll be fine. Look forward to the organization claiming the very same player's hockey heritage as the reason for success when they make it big.

Navigation Tip: Just like calling in sick to go to a job interview at a prospective company, it is incumbent on you to stress to your player to keep his/her plans to himself. Don't post any travels on social media and turn off any GPS locators. Those darn kids and their apps.

Depending on your budget and your kid's appetite for change, you can expect a variety of results from these decisions. Nobody can guarantee success. Here are some examples of outcomes:

- Player goes to a prestigious prep school their freshman year. Parents fork over $65K/year only to find out they need to spend another $65K to cover the 5th year also known as PG (Post-Grad) year. Education is pretty good, the kid gets a D1 commitment and plays in the North American Hockey League with hopes of spending only 2 years there without injury. No guarantees for NCAA commitment until they sign the NLI (National Letter of Intent).
- Player wants to play up a level (in the US, this is at age 15). Gets hurt half-way through the season because he's way too skinny to be playing Hulk-smash hockey. Gets drafted to a USHL team before his 16th year, college commitment, gets hurt again, USHL team doesn't keep him and plays in the BCHL hoping to play college if he can remain injury-free.
- Player goes to Study/Train/Play Hockey school that takes place in a conference room at a rink. He gets a phenomenal GPA based on online schooling. It's easy to

cheat, I mean...learn online. We know that these credits are good for college but we have no idea if they learn anything substantive to prepare them for college level classes, just a few marketing pamphlets saying they will. Ice and off-ice training is offered, but they are stuck in a room with only hockey players of various ages while in high school. Bummer social setting, definitely lacks diversity and benefits of class participation. A means to the end.

- Player moves across the country to billet. Finds out they are the family's hired babysitter and the billet family does not eat nutrition-dense food. Player resorts to DoorDash in order to eat enough calories to maintain his weight. Hockey is fine but player is homesick and can't wait to go home when the season is over.
- Player has an awesome hockey experience and wonderful billet family who adopts him for life. Online high school mixed with TikTok viewership and mastering Xbox. Maybe homesick if too young, depends on the kid and if the parents fly out for games.
- Player moves across the country to billet, hardly plays and gets cut after the first season. Hey, they get an A for effort! Nothing ventured, nothing gained.
- Player moves to hockey academy which is neither a prep school or a high school but rather a hockey frat house where players attend a private school or take classes online. All depends on who the horse wrangler is. Are they a good person? Do they follow protocols for SafeSport? Just ask alot of questions and trust your gut instincts.
- Player moves to another team in another state, parents move with him, selling their house and leaving their friends. Coach made some promises that he couldn't keep, but hey! Hopefully they made some money for college on that real estate deal!

- Player is quietly considering a move to another team and accidentally shares with a teammate. Teammate announces his plans in a group Xbox game and it magically gets back to the organization. Loyalty is questioned and an insidious threat to blackball ensues.
- Some prep schools require repeating a year in high school if coming in after freshman year. The school claims it best for the education of the student athlete and some other bogus requirements. They just want another year of prep school money but if you don't like it, you can leave. There's a sucker born every minute.

These are scenarios based on true stories, and there are thousands. However, there are many success stories too! In the military, they say "Embrace the Suck" referring to mental toughness. Working hard, having discipline and overcoming adversity in whatever form that looks like is part of the hockey/sports journey. For every set of crummy circumstances, there is another set of positive outcomes. For every bad actor, there is usually (not always) a karma bitch-slap of what goes around comes around. All I'm saying is that parents hope for the best and seem surprised when they have no ability to plan for the worst.

Plan B is usually real-time, whether it's hiring a mental performance coach or gritting it out, the player needs to feel supported. Try not to shit on your kid, it's very important for them to navigate their journey even if you don't agree with their thought process. *As parents, we can get cognitively trapped in our ways of dealing with things.* If you embrace the role of a mountain guide, you're carrying the bullshit weight and encouraging the trek forward. However, sometimes you need to simply pause and turn around until it's the right time to ascend. The climb is for the athlete, they need to do it! The key is balancing support with a bit of pragmatism. If they want to keep going, they'll keep going.

And....it gets even dicier when the kids get into the juniors as they think they're going to a certain town to play on the team that drafted them but can be cut or traded in a moment's notice. It may be another year in the juniors, despite being led to believe they are going to play in the college they planned for. Nothing is forever in hockey. Parents at this level say it stops being fun "parenting" at this stage. More heartache and stress at the junior levels, but sometimes complete euphoria that erases all of it, depends on the day!

Navigation Tip: Shoot for the stars. But parents need to have a Plan B renting out space in the back of your mind.

These kids are living their dream and if they just work hard, believe in themselves and never give up, they will get somewhere. Even if it ends up being club hockey or beer league, it never hurts to try. Optimism with a Plan B. It is why the pizza is so good in Naples, Italy where they live under the constant threat of Mt. Vesuvius erupting. Eat as if it's your last meal, but just know, you could be buried in ash by tomorrow, so have an escape route just in case. Or just stay in the moment and enjoy your delicious pizza.

Back to my original analogy, there is no Hockey Rumspringa because the organization guides the flow of money and what is best for building an attractive organization, not what's actually best for that individual player.

WARNING: Mama Bear rant ahead...(if you call me a Karen, I'll knock your block off - I learned something from NY Hockey mom.)

Seriously fellas: we pay you. If it weren't for us, you would not be making a living. Since when does a kid who is 15 years old have all the answers? Since when does a mom or dad who just want to see their kid get a fair shake at the options deserve any less than a chance to explore those options? It's like moving on in any career, if you're in a dead-end job, you look elsewhere. Kids should be encouraged to apply without fear of retribution, much like we encourage them to apply to multiple colleges in case the dream doesn't work out. If you provide a "safe space" free of threats and fear, you may actually get a team who wants to stay together, regardless of what else is out there. If you're so worried about how it affects the team, then spend less time scaring everyone and more time recruiting the kids that want to be on your team. Development first, business second. It's the way players advance, don't always blame the parents on this one. Have some skin in the game so we don't all lose our shirts.

As a team manager for two years, I had gotten too close to the guts of how hockey organizations operate. You strike up conversations with other team managers between games, comparing war stories of parents, coaches and the politics of bullshit. Too bad there wasn't a GlassDoor for teams but I'd fear it would only be disgruntled parents complaining about ice time. Organizations are like big universities, if you pay your bill and are likely to return, you are a good investment. Hockey organizations say things like, "follow the process" and "it's not a sprint, it's a marathon" and "stay with the group, we have so many successful players at the next level, we'll help you get there." Meanwhile they are busy marketing to the next crop of players. Watch the social media sites, the NHL draft pick that played in your organization for one season when they were 10. In general, they aren't getting involved with the day-to-day feedback because they really don't want to open up Pandora's box, it's better to spout out motivational hockey quotes than address quiet rumblings of legitimate concerns, all under the guise of "mental toughness." Ouch. Embrace the suck.

Some parents declare that their player is definitely coming back the next year, others stay silent. It's like a giant game of "Clue" because on the surface, everyone is chummy but underneath, there's an escape route in case of a better opportunity. Absolute secrecy, because if anyone finds out you are looking to leave or are starting talks with another team (prep school, Detroit), you're dead to them. Again, watch out for Tony Soprano's henchmen on this, they come around with innocent questions only to let it slip in conversation getting back to the coach. Watch out for the moles, could be a coach from another team. A skills coach. One big happy family.

We took a chance in January 2020, oblivious to the upcoming dream-crusher called Covid. We flew incognito to an east coast prep school, ranked in the top 5. Coaches had an impressive track record and were highly regarded by players and families. My son and I talked to his hockey advisor on how to prepare for the interview (dress code, firm handshake, prepared questions and other tips on how to nail an interview). This was great practice for the real world, so there's that! He met with admissions, we toured the school with a hockey player, and then it was time to suit up and practice with the current team. A few kids "knew" him by looking up his stats but after an hour of practice, they welcomed the lone wolf into the pack as he skated fast, nailed the drills and hit the net almost every time. The kid was prepared and ready to move to another team. He was motivated.

Considering a prep school involves finding a magic crystal ball and a small inheritance. Don't have either of those? We leaned on the hockey advisor. Not sure that was worth the money, but he was the only person outside our bubble, and he knew the coach at the prep school. Again, complete secrecy. He advised that moving east was better for our son. He used terms like gaining better exposure, more playing opportunities and meshing with college-bound student athletes. My son was not interested in skating with a team in Detroit, as others had done that with mixed reviews (we learned about this after Covid). It involved billeting and breaking into what felt like another universe made up of tribal connections that we had not made. I've never been to the swamp but there may be some deep state hockey out there. No thanks. Prep school, despite the price, felt safer in terms of education and walking distance to a rink. Prep school hockey games along the east coast are within shorter driving distances. The costs were expensive but fixed and exuded a sense of overall wellness based on our research. Also exuded country club attitudes, but hey, maybe someone has a nice place on the Cape we could rent. He was sad about leaving "the boys" but was feeling pigeonholed and ready to move on. New coaches. A step forward for development.

After crunching the numbers, I knew I needed to dust off my resume and find a full-time job. My trailer home side hustle was cute, but not enough cash if we wanted to travel and see some of those games. Oh yeah, and pay our mortgage. We had another son in college and a young daughter still at home. Our oldest son was self-sufficient, so yay! Hubby's paycheck went to the home finances, not these oppressive bills hijacked by the hockey juniper plant.

I remember writing the parent statement that was required for my son's application to the prep school. Some cathartic moments writing that parent statement. Approaching 50 years of age, my window of "I give a shit" was starting to close. I was constantly fighting the urge to be negative and instead making my life goal to avoid f-bombing before 7:30 a.m. I don't know what I wrote, but it was less crazy hockey mom talk and more about wanting a higher quality education and reducing carbon emissions by being in one place. Good schmooze.

Navigation Tip: Take a breath. Go back to church. Not religious? Meditate. And don't be afraid to ask yourself, what is happening to me? Why am I always so angry?

Hockey wears you down as a parent. Waking up at 3:30 am in the morning with anxiety. The extreme highs and lows, scary financial decisions that are intertwined with a sincere belief that your player can actually do it. You base this belief on their work ethic and unwavering passion and drive. You need to get out of their way and encourage the climb. Mountain guide mindset without letting the winter goggles get scratched and fogged (like considering cashing out a Roth IRA to pay for stuff). You will second-guess the route but eventually pack the bag.

Consulting everyone's gut-instinct, we went for it. We had all grown tired of the grind of keeping up with academics and long hours spent in the car just to get to practice. My son was ready to start fresh, earn his spot on another team and establish himself. My husband and I became numb to the numbers, just like paying for good sleep by upgrading from Econolodge to a Hampton Inn. Sure, why not, I'll pay an extra $40 for a better pillow and a cleaner bathroom. Hockey Rumspringa! Game on.

Remember, it's the noise around this sport that creates the stress. I have a friend who is a scout for the NFL. He said there are a lot of similarities between football and hockey except that in football, some of the toughest kids came from humble beginnings, not prep schools. This is true of some hockey players too, I remember hearing a story about former Blackhawks player Artemi Panerin from Russia. With handmade hockey gloves and second-hand equipment, by the time he was 8 years-old he was practicing 6 times a week. He was bullied for his poverty and was cut from the best team at age 13. He wanted to quit, but his work ethic produced an escape route from poverty. When he finally had new equipment, he was a force to be reckoned with. Hockey was not only his passion, but a way out. He proved himself to others, and he made it to the pros and is a superstar.

In the US, the price tag that comes with playing hockey is no joke. My son's godparents from Chicago, who happen to be African-American, asked us if any black kids played the sport. They were his biggest fans, cheering him on anytime we traveled to Chicago, making posters and standing up in the bleachers anytime he had the puck. I could only recall a few guys in the pros, sort of looking down at my feet when answering that diversity is not something on the lips of many learn to skate programs yet.

Exposure camps, scouting reports, off-season invitations all affect decisions that are made on the journey. Family advisors are good at marketing and sometimes players are led to believe their own press, despite the stats. That could be both a curse and a blessing. In one way, they are confident because of it or they have a false sense of security. Words from the wild shout "they will find you" if you are good. Emails and Twitter accounts from coaches, hockey experts on how to contact college coaches or reciting the broken record on how important it is to keep a great GPA if you are attempting the DI college route. Just keep your head on straight, there are a lot of people looking to money grab and institute their predator ways on your kids' innocent and pure love for the sport. The odds are tough. There are more than enough junior and semi-pro leagues out there that each have their own successes. The key is looking at the odds, and considering what they mean for your family.

We put down our $10K deposit on prep school in early March 2020. Covid was something happening in China and Italy. Whatever! We have smart people in the US who would stop it from getting to us, geez! We told the coach for the next year we were jumping ship. Felt really good.

Wait....Wait, what's that? An Avalanche!

By April 15, we pleaded for our money back as the future of hockey in the fall was unknown. Thanks, Covid. Coinciding with the abyss of the unknown, we also learned that both prep school coaches (who loved how my son played) accepted jobs for a USHL team. Then another hockey team recruited all the best players from that very same prep school team to a hockey academy/hybrid high school. Some vengeance Tony Soprano stuff going on there that we were oblivious to. I can't make this shit up. What was left on that team were a few stragglers and a goalie. *Poof!* I started chanting "everything happens for a reason" as I put on my favorite sweatpants and never knew what day it was for the next 6 months.

None of the hockey teams played in USA Hockey's National Championship that year. Our team was slated to go. Our advisor was just as stunned and shocked as we were, everyone questioned whether there would BE a hockey season as some states were using ice rinks as morgues.

Feeling panicky, depressed and a little angry, we decided to walk it back to our local team. One step above groveling, my son had an uneasy feeling about the upcoming season. His teammates were happy to have him back and chided him for trying to leave, promising to haze him when he least expected it. Perhaps some clear tape on the blades of his skates, ink in the chin guard, loose cap on the water bottle or falling for another Deez Nuts joke. My husband and I were happy that he still had a hockey home but also felt uneasy as his "loyalty" to the team was tarnished.

Tryouts happened, he made the team despite the fact that a few players from the fourth line were cut. Extra awkward because they walked out through the parking lot where everyone was told to wait for their players because of Covid concerns. The new coaches that year were also former NHL players. The assistant coach had an impressive coaching experience in his background and just so happened to have a son on the team. The Lexus lane was already feeling congested before we signed our first check, I could feel the fear-and-loathing of facing adversity. The head coach had a career-ending injury and managed to squeeze in one year of coaching before our team inherited him. He seemed to have a strange personality where he could not make eye contact with parents and seemed to fixate on his own rags-to-riches story. He repeated stories and mantras like Rain Man, but he knew hockey. With new rules on the pandemic horizon, it was an ominous start to a new coaching relationship within a global pandemic.

In late May, the USHL draft was still on as scheduled, with a nationwide online presence. For the USHL draft, a player at the ripe old age of 15 can get drafted. Most of these draft picks come from the most competitive teams. Most, not all, of the kids who played up a level get drafted. There was still a sense of unfinished business as USA Hockey Nationals had been canceled, depleting the scouting circus one last time before the draft.

The top 1% have a shot of making the National Team Development Program (NTDP). These are the players who have been placed on a list early in the season, normally tryouts would cast a wider net before a final roster is set up. If a player is good enough to make it, they are likely to be named to the initial NHL Central Scouting Rankings by the time they are 17. In 2020, there were not any

NTDP tryouts, and instead they released the roster on who would be playing for the Under 17 team.

As for the USHL draft, what your advisor is supposed to do is create a bio sheet on your player, hob-knob with the various team scouts while watching games and have a by-line answer for what makes your player different. There is a lot of "Don't you worry, nothing to see here" hand-waving going on. If your advisor is any good, he's already had the rink-side chats with teams that perhaps have expressed interest on the down-low. We learned this after-the-fact, our guys were Missing In Action when we asked about this, I guess they had something better to do.

What is important is to have your kid practice *how* to essentially interview with a scout who calls you before the draft. We did not know of this practice, so he was very surprised. There are a lot of tips and tricks that go a long way. Example questions are as follows:

- What are your goals?
- What do you want to study in college?
- What are your strengths?
- Who do you model your style to in the NHL?
- What do you need to work on?
- What are your plans for summer?
- Do you have any questions?

All of these questions, my kid answered with the most brevity possible on the first call. I spied on him while he was talking. I'm not sure he opened his mouth any wider than if he was trying to spit a sunflower seed out while talking. Answered that he liked science a lot. He managed to squeak out something about being an explosive skater. Funny enough, this was what the scout said to him in the first statement, we really like your explosive skating and stick-handling. No questions, just said thank you and hung up.

On the second call, he was a little better. In any case, he may have bombed the interviews, but my guess is that most 15-year old hockey players have not mastered the art of nailing an interview. Later in the day, he got a call from the new coach of the 16's who somehow became the middle man fielding calls from interested teams. Not sure why he was point-man, given that he didn't really know our son. We just went with the flow which had felt like a daunting, mystical process.

One by one, several of his teammates were drafted, kids he had been playing with on his own line and in power plays....but his name did not appear. We sent congratulatory texts to the families. Names of players he had played with at Nationals the summer before, recognizing tournament players from other "elite" tournaments over the years all of which deserved to be on those lists despite a few surprises. Feeling deflated but optimistic, he waited for the second day of the draft. It was possible to still be drafted; the second day is customarily the older birth years, a few kids who were passed over the year before, had phenomenal 16U years, and those 17's and 18's who played in prep schools or blossomed later get named. Then it's over.

No dice.

This is where the advisor came in after the fact, a bit apologetic but also unfazed by his sadness. As a family, we were disappointed because we had not felt prepared for either outcome. We paid these guys to manage our expectations and do their part. We trusted them and felt like suckers. In retrospect, we were technically in the same boat as any family who did not have a hockey advisor, so really shouldn't have expected anything. Just because we paid for representation doesn't mean he deserved it any more than the kid who was a free agent. Your kid didn't make it, so what? Pull up the boot-straps and recover. It's part of life! Embrace the suck, right? Ask any professional athlete, many of them can attest to setbacks and recovery. Maybe it was size, maybe it was grit. Maybe he didn't hold the door open, or the coach said something negative. We'll never know why because there is not a single person you can ask. A mystical process. At least on American Idol, they give the contestant the reason why they are not moving on. The truth can set you free, right?

Ok, so now the post-mortem of not getting drafted. What's next?

For the player, they still need to process how they truly feel, and it comes in waves. First anger, then feeling deflated, then determined, then insecure, then angry again and determined again. If I made a cake as a symbol in that moment, it would have sad-mad ingredients smothered with frosting made of resolve.

A couple of days later, he started receiving emails with invites for USHL main camps and prospect camps, so he was on some lists. Some were deemed TBA based on how that state was interpreting health and safety recommendations due to Covid. It was a bit of a boost in the hockey psyche despite all of the unknowns due to the pandemic. Regardless, he knew he had to find a way to use available resources to meet this new set of challenges.

I had a bunch of weights in the basement and a stationary bike, so he contacted his trainer and set up his own workouts. Reminded me of the movies where the prisoner gets ripped in their jail cell by doing pushups and situps.

He discovered boxing workouts and golf. He reorganized the garage and created new stickhandling drills. He slipped into the backdoors of ice rinks that took cash in order to stay afloat despite Covid lockdowns. Hockey players can't just "stop." Gymnasts are similar, they only take two weeks off the entire year. The hockey kids were watching NHL players stickhandle in their kitchens on social media. No shortage of TikTok videos on how to make steak properly, learn about the newest fads and watching girls perform the latest dance trends that entertained the male teenage brain. If it weren't for hockey and his friends on the team, he would have been a statistic in the massive wave of teenage depression.

These guys all kept at it, never losing sight of their commitment to the dream. They consistently communicated through group chats and wore their chin diapers (masks) when they saw each other. As parents wrung their hands in worry about getting sick, these boys figured out how to survive a pandemic by adapting to changes in circumstances. No days off mentality. No shortage of chirps on who was getting fat or breaking up with a girlfriend, their community was stronger than ever and had evolved into something none of us could have directed as parents. As a sherpa, I could sit this one out. They were bushwhacking their own route as a group without any help from the parents or coaches.

He attended two USHL camps that summer, made it all the way to the final games, and reset his parameters. Those camps were incredible. Watching the live-streams, it was obvious that there was a big difference between the 16 year-olds and the 19 year-olds who were fighting for their hockey life. Comparing yourself to others is inevitable, some players were so good that it was inconceivable they were not yet on the team roster. Humbling.

They say that people who are happiest have a dream, have defined goals and put a plan together to reach their goals. The 49 times an actress auditions, then becomes an academy award winner. The comedian who hustles for years performing the club circuit at late night bars, bombing their act until they get it right. The NFL player who had his hand amputated at the age of 4 but still went to football training with his twin brother and ended up playing in the NFL. The human spirit, one with perseverance and unwavering belief in a dream is capable of doing almost anything.

12

BROKEN STICKS

avigation Tip:

N *avigation Tip:*
Activate your intuition when doing your research during the Rumspringa to look for new teams. Find good coaches with multiple references, talk to the parents.

The Red Hot Chili Peppers almost did not release the song "Under the Bridge" because Anthony Kiedis, the band's lead singer, did not think it was a good fit. The song had some dark lyrics based on his life experiences and he felt it was too emotional for the band's style. He ended up writing happy chords to balance out the sadness and the song is one of the band's most memorable pieces of work. It was important to tell his story.

This chapter is about the broken sticks that, despite the investment, snapped after the warranty expired. I'll try not to make this too salty for you. However, it is too important to leave out for fear of bumming anyone out, so look for the sweetness to swallow the jagged little pill.

Overcoming adversity is an understatement. These stories will leave you with the feeling of disgust similar to being inside a changing room in Wal-Mart, looking at the mirror, and noticing that hail damage on your butt cheeks from 30 years of eating cheese fries. It ain't pretty. Girls, you get me. Guys, it's comparable to the Molson muscle and no...the chicks do not dig it.

I interviewed parents of kids from sports besides hockey. Basketball, lacrosse, gymnastics, and soccer also seem to attract some douchebag coaches. Real peaches. These parents approached me because they wanted their story heard by someone. It appears there is no shortage out there of arrogance without much to back it up. Some folks are emboldened by positions of power, dodging the attention of anyone other than the one or two kids who are silently dealing with some level of emotional abuse. It can be insidious and small without any symptoms, it can also be very painful much like a case of the clap until somebody quits and the disease is staved off.

I observed the following patterns in my conversations with heartbroken parents:

1. The Promise
2. The Showing
3. The Targeting
4. The Punishment and Threat
5. The Denial

Aside from a standard background check, coaches are required to take a few training classes to get certified, none of which prevents those with a propensity for cruelty from sneaking in. Some seasons are worse than others, depending on what is going on in that person's life that year.

Some situations were unclear and could be categorized as existing within "shades of gray." Not every tough coach is sadistic or ill-intentioned. Only a few are well-versed in what it takes to inspire the next generation of athletes. Somewhere in the gray areas, a kid's sport psyche can be manipulated and damaged. Those who experienced coach-related setbacks leveraged their situation as motivation to flourish in the next phase of their development. Others tapped out, often referring to the coach as a personality type to avoid in future personal or professional relationships. A few got lost in their thoughts and struggled with damaged self-worth.

How did some families get into these precarious situations? Didn't they do the research? Did they not check references, talk to other parents or do the mandatory gut-check? Were they gas-lighted? Did they simply base their decision on good faith and great marketing? Let's dive in with our collective consciousness and explore before we judge the next parent as a "Karen" or "Ken" when they report something to SafeSport.

For those that don't know, SafeSport[1] is a non-profit organization established under the Protecting Young Victims from Sexual Abuse and Safe Sport Authorization Act of 2017. The intention is to provide training for coaches, laden with rules and policies for preventing emotional, physical and sexual abuse and misconduct. It is also an administrative body that receives reports of abuse, deciding when to investigate a complaint based on certain criteria. If they deem it necessary, they respond and take action.

For hockey players, there is an unwritten rule that hockey "tough" means tolerating some negativity. It's what makes you mentally resilient. Locker room talk can also be brutal, it is part of the appeal. When a coach is tough, teammates figure out a way to please him/her by working harder and smarter. They learn to win and lose as a team. Similarly, other sports have codes that produce phenomenal athletes who endured tough coaching and came out on top. There are coaches who earn a player's respect because of the way they use psychology alongside constructive criticism. There are books, training and seminars on these topics, but ultimately a coach is going to have a baseline of how they "grew up" with the sport. So if they experienced negative reinforcement coaching and persevered, there is a possibility they will resort to similar tactics. Not always the case, but I'm never surprised to learn that so-and-so had a mentor who was quasi-sadistic.

As a society, we can subconsciously think our kids are the future Navy Seals whose motto is "I persevere and thrive on adversity. My

Nation expects me to be physically harder and mentally stronger than my enemies. If knocked down, I will get back up, every time." It's just that, well, the Navy Seals chose to endure one of the most brutal regimens on the planet and accepted that only a small number will actually complete it.

Just spit-balling here, but the frontal lobe for the average teen's brain isn't fully developed until their mid-20s. Rational thinking is still, meh. They process emotions in a different part of their brain (the amygdala) and the two brain parts don't really sync up for a while. Throw in some active-shooter drills in school starting in kindergarten. Social media. Climate change. Playing a sport is supposed to be an escape from it all.

As kids excel in their sport, they must maintain a focus on physical and mental health. They don't always have the tools, so their guardian needs to step in. I think of my early parenting days when I had to send my older sons to daycare five times a week. I settled on a place that we could afford and gave it a trial run. Looking back, the place was like a 1980s Romanian orphanage, kids lined up in cribs in the infant room, some crying the entire time I was on the tour. After flipping through fancy brochures and talking to a few parents who were happy with the daycare, I asked the director why so many of the toddlers were crying and she said it was a bad time to visit because it was their nap time. There were not that many places that had openings we could afford, so we settled with this one. I left my two little boys on the first day with a guarded trust that they would be properly cared for. Later that week, I returned to find my oldest son with a sizable bite mark on his arm and the other son had developed a horrible diaper rash. They could not tell me how or why either happened, so I immediately removed them without question. Shortly thereafter, I found a wonderful place with two openings. It was a good fit and I trusted the staff after my version of the Spanish inquisition. To this day, my older boys periodically reveal their repressed memories of day care days, mostly about having to eat lumpy oatmeal and singing a ridiculous amount of songs. One son is now a professional chef and the other sings in his own rock band. Hmmmm. I digress.

For those who send their players on to prep schools, there is an implicit understanding that teachers, coaches and administrators have the student's best interests at heart when making decisions affecting their futures. Although it can feel like a white collar prison at times, the student athletes are expected to follow the rules and they will develop new skills for sport and in life. For those who keep their student athlete at home, sending them to practice 15-20 hours a week at a facility, there is an agreement that the coach will train the athlete with skills and behavior modifications to improve their game. Somewhere in there, they should have fun and enjoy their youth.

As parents, we learn to rely on the experts telling us what is "best" for athletes taking it to the next level. Logically, we turn to professionals, websites, advisors, podcasts, and other parents. We challenge our intuition and make decisions based on stats: winning records, number of years coaching, and impressive bios. We start to believe the press that a program is good based on a myriad of factors with intuition often buried in the promise of a Mercedes of a program.

1. The Promise:

When an athlete has outgrown their present situation or gets cut from a team, new opportunities come up. Perhaps the player was recruited by a coach who saw them play. A period of flattery and feedback can boost the athlete's confidence and have them believing they have a shot if given the chance. A place to play that will be good for him/her. The program director or coach may describe the training regimen and provide a list of those that have made it to the next level in the sport. They may say things like, "we are unique" and "we have it all."

JOIN US.

Perhaps they have a newer program or have moved into a different league, looking to recruit some new talent. This could be code for supplementing income for players who cannot afford to play, oftentimes becoming the unwitting sugar daddy for the team. Or maybe they have some talent and just need your player to be part of the giant stick-and-puck for their new superstars.

Perhaps they have a spokesperson who has street cred, a successful professional sports background or has worked with them on other projects. This spokesperson is someone who can vouch for the program. Lending their name to something that is new or hopeful seems like a good sign.

Consider yourself unlucky if it starts with promising a Mercedes and you get the Ford Pinto.

2. The Showing:

Perhaps an area is staged well. They have a fancy landing page for their website, a nice workout facility and other perks that most reputable sports programs have. There may be a new practice area or specialty coaches who come in to help train. The school may have a winning record in that sport, sending athletes on to college programs. There is a fair amount of welcoming and handshakes, kids doing their homework or working on some type of drill as you pass by. Maybe you are shown a trophy case of past accomplishments. This is the marketing and sales phase of the process. Sniff sniff, does anything smell like bullshit yet? Maybe not.

3. The Targeting:

Kids who feel targeted by their coach oftentimes don't complain to anyone about it. At the higher levels, they are hungry to develop their skills and want to play their sport. There is an awareness that the parents have made some sacrifices to get them there, so whining about a mean coach is not in their vernacular. Regardless of whether they are away or close to home, they are spending countless hours in practice. Surviving is different from thriving, so rather than being seen as "soft," the kid learns to be submissive. They always need to talk to their coach and ask for feedback, parents are not involved.

Targeting is when the kid or a small subset of the team are singled out without any apparent justification. Sometimes they're humiliated in front of their teammates, directly or on the sidelines. It's a pattern that reflects a thousand tiny cuts rather than one kill shot. Perhaps the player was promised something, a starting position or help in getting connected with the coach's buddy who runs a program at the next level. Variables are endless, but there is always a promise followed up with a harshness that feels, well, not right.

Being benched for an errant comment, not executing a play, or missing a practice are all within acceptable boundaries to keep discipline on the bench. When it gets tricky is when the athlete knows the coach does not like them for some reason and they blame themselves. If the athlete asks the coach to work with them, they are given generic reasons why they are not excelling that don't necessarily jibe. The coach may even rationalize it by offering an apology, stating, "Sorry I was hard on you yesterday, but...." Again, gray areas abound because perspectives change based on performance and wins. It's not a perfect science.

4. The Punishment and the Threats:

Another gray area. Perhaps the kid is tasked with menial labor or benched despite a great performance. Perhaps a teammate makes the same mistakes and is never reprimanded. Or the athlete does exactly what is asked of them by their coach and is still flawed despite all of their best efforts. I have seen players transfer to other teams mid-season because of this, the coach did not like the way they played and the player just never felt valued. I have heard of players "sticking it out" the entire season, having the guts to keep moving forward after being systematically berated by their coach.

Punishments can come in different forms too.

There are coaches who purposely dangle, but never act on, promises to talk to their connections at colleges or other teams as a reward. There are coaches who will contact prospective teams to smear the reputation of the athlete, noting character flaws or work ethic as a reason. Coaches who shame the athlete and demand complete obedience to the point where the athlete cannot discuss anything with the coach for fear of reprimand. Fear of failure.

A friend of mine had a competitive gymnast in her family. The coach would make comparisons to teammates that made her believe she was inferior and would never amount to their level of skill. The parents said their daughter excelled in her sport despite what the coach had said, medaling in most of her events. She had started harming herself, hiding the cuts, and eventually attempted suicide. She had been in an almost cult-like relationship with her teammates and coach, spending upwards of 30 hours a week in practice without much oversight. Yeah, we know all kinds of crazy exists in *THAT* sport.

What about a basketball player? Colleges were looking at their son, he had all the makings of a DI player. The coach had recruited him to play on his high school team. Over the course of two years, a boy who had started as a toddler with the Fisher Price basketball game needed to quit his senior year. There were signs, coaching decisions that didn't make sense given his performance. He was not the coach's favorite player and, despite having half the minutes on the court in one season, he had the most points. Each time he was admonished, he fought back by assisting and scoring while staying humble.

Then one day, the coach just locked him out of the gym because he went to fill his water bottle after he had finished his drills. Rather than nurture the positive growth, there was a pattern of emotional and verbal abuse. Never in front of adults, rarely in front of assistant coaches and mostly done in private conversations with the kid. When separated from the herd, he jumped on his vulnerability. Seems so minor, but according to his parents, there was a pattern of quiet jabs from this coach right before games.

Things like:

- "You are not good enough to make college ball."
- "I don't know who you think you are, but I'm not playing you next game if you make that mistake again."
- "You think you're hot shit, think again."
- "You don't even want to be here, do you."

The kid quit. He went into college not knowing what he did wrong and ended up floundering for a few years, dabbling in drugs and depression. When he got some talk therapy, he was advised to go back and watch the videos of his old games as a way to help him heal. What he realized was that he was good. Really good. He could see how happy he was in his earlier years and that gradually, his smile disappeared despite making the winning shot in overtime at the state championship game. He now coaches basketball at his old high school and is revered by the parents and kids.

5. The Denial

This one really sticks in my craw, especially when there are multiple complaints. Despite an overt set of threats or punishment, the coach and maybe organization protecting them, will sometimes defend their actions to avoid tarnishing their reputation or their school's reputation. SafeSport has enough sexual allegations and physical abuse to deal with, the gray areas are more challenging to investigate. Unless you have coaches wearing body cams, the kid is going to have to figure out how to clear up issues directly with their coach. If they can't resolve it directly, then they need to feel as if they can discuss it with their parents. If the kid is keeping things quiet but there is some intuitive hint, then you must act. Some of these coaches are despised but the players don't want anything to kill their dream so they stay silent. Powerless. Again, it can be complicated and messy without an exact definition, but it happens. It builds character and it happens more than we think. Consider yourself lucky if you get through the sports years without a megalomaniac.

Here's the replay, ask yourself if your athlete is:

- Confident.
- Supported.
- Having fun.
- A good teammate.
- Following the rules.
- Making attempts to discuss the sticky issues with the coach and can advocate for themselves.
- Showing any signs of duress (school, relationships, self-esteem or losing weight).

And read some books on this stuff if you are apprehensive. I'm not a psychiatrist. I'm merely suggesting that it's important to stop and assess periodically. Once I started talking about this book I was writing in casual conversation, people came out of the woodwork to talk about their experiences. As guides, it is intentionally hiking through a big storm that can harm your child. In Colorado, when you set out to climb a mountain that is 14,000+ feet, you check the weather, and if you can't get down before the storm hits, you don't go.

It is important to not feel like "THAT" parent or "THOSE" parents because that parent is not necessarily you. Remember that.

On that note, just actively listen and be prepared to say "no" to a program if your hackles go up. It is usually a sign that something isn't right.

13

BIG YEAR AND NATTY'S

T he U16 year for competitive hockey teams is a big year. It feels like a "make or break" year for kids as it represents a decision point for many. The small group that is drafted to the NTDP or ready to play in the Canadian Hockey League (CHL) are severed from the fray of youth hockey. This distinct group of players have their own competitive hurdles and play in the next level of the junior league. The players devote their entire day to hockey development and generally have an elite skill set where going to the NHL is in their realm of possibilities. So the Lexus lane exits and the funnel of opportunities narrows. Plenty of hockey years ahead of U16, but to the kids at the beginning of a U16 season, they consider it a critical year.

Navigation Tip: The pantheon of the all-time hockey greats did not all get drafted to the juniors in their U16 season (Midget). There is still time, but it is a pivotal year for the top-level prospects. There are dozens of junior leagues varying in levels throughout the US and Canada. Plenty of feeder leagues with opportunities to advance. Try to relax if this year is not the banner year.

∾

The fall of 2020 was filled with confusion for much of the world. Schools moved classes online, the Covid vaccines were not widely available and mask-wearing was a political issue. The NHL playoffs began in August and concluded in September, having been postponed like most sports. Athletic programs in high school were halted. Some college programs did not play. As to checkbook hockey? We found a way.

- Our team practiced.
- Our team played.
- Our team was asked to spend $125/kid for a Covid test anytime we traveled.
- Coaches got sick, the entire team would quarantine for 14 days.
- Team flew to Minnesota, found out the goalie tested positive; the team flew home without spending the night.
- Hockey parents had mixed opinions on what was right and wrong.
- We fell into group-think, negotiating with our better angels and wishing for wellness.

Tournaments were held in the red states. Wisconsin, North Dakota, Nebraska, and Texas. Emergency rooms were filled with Covid patients, we prayed that nobody got a concussion or a broken bone in the games.

I felt guilty anytime my son took the car to pick up his teammate and drive to practice. The normal hockey boogers and coughs were now considered "the Rona." We didn't really talk about it out of fear of being judged by others. I would see pictures of the boys all sitting side-by-side at the gates in the airport terminal wearing the masks on their chins. They shared hotel rooms, dinners, locker rooms and germs as if nothing had changed. At the time, it felt rebellious and irreverent. And careless.

It also kept a subset of the population distracted from the world's problems. The parents watched their kids on livestream or traveled if they could. The boys never stopped training as this was simply an inconvenience. From the standpoint of mental health, it was the best thing for them as they were able to thrive in a period of our history that will forever be stained by political divisiveness, sickness and death. For hockey players who were fortunate enough to play through it, they will forever remember the importance of the U16 season.

As mentioned earlier in the book, it was not as much fun but more like competing for a promotion or a job. We had a coach who pushed the limits of rational thinking. The boys bonded, they got through the madness, honed their strengths and did what they needed to do. They worked their asses off and made it to the USA Hockey Nationals tournament. This was their third year qualifying with the core group of players.

I didn't have the will to travel most of the season. I didn't want to get sick or deal with all of the restrictions on spectators. When this team was U14, they lost in the first round and headed home happy that they got to participate. The U15 year was canceled. This time, it was different. It was the "pivotal" year.

With my years as team manager in the rear view mirror, I knew I had to see him play so I packed my suitcase. I had to review the essentials for a week of potential games. Thinking through all of the possible weather changes, needing the obligatory winter hat, workout clothes and gym shoes, laptop, phone charger, warm clothes and travel sized toiletries, middle-aged woman supplements and flex-band for my physical therapy exercises. I was tattered, cynical, and a little bit worn down like my winter boots at the end of a hockey season. Salt stains, rough edges and broken in. I know there are hockey families that are on their third kid which means their entire adult life has circulated around this sport.

One of my friends was on her fifth child playing hockey, her 16-year old baby was the last one out. Her kids were genetically blessed with perfect hockey physique, had a strong Christian faith and oozed "hard working." They had achieved the highest levels of play in the sport, with a tough love drive that spilled from one sibling to the next. From what I heard, it was the third born (and only female) who was the toughest and most disciplined, playing DI in the women's hockey program. Her brothers credited her with having the best hockey smarts and despite the glass ceiling for women's hockey, she had earned everyone's respect. One day over coffee, I was amazed to learn that this hockey mom had spent the better of 25 years shuttling kids to and from hockey practices and larger events. Hockey saint, quiet and unassuming but a master at navigating the crazy and talking to the scouts. She was a farm mom. Her kids never talked back and they called her "Ma."

Navigation Tip: Absorb each moment and relish every relationship you have with team parents this year. This will likely be the last time all of these players will be together. At the end of this season, most move on and a few stop playing. Your connections gradually become digital.

Speaking of a higher being and faith, I frequently found myself praying when my son was not having a great game, making deals with God that I would volunteer more if he could just score a goal in this period. I recruited my mom to start praying on demand. Being a devout Catholic she would simply skip down the line from Jesus and go directly to St. Anthony for a favor. St. Anthony is known as the Patron Saint of lost items and somehow became a perfect imitation for Jesus. "Tony Tony come around, find a goal 'cuz it cannot be found." The patron saint of hockey. Boom, he'd score.

Superstition in sports is a natural phenomena. Why do we sit in the stands next to certain people and if the game is not going right, you have to change the mojo and move somewhere else? Maybe you need to stand, maybe you need to sit two bleachers up, maybe you need to move to the rink-side to the right of the goalie, or need to pace. There are so many ways you can drum up your protective or magic role to ease the burden of somehow determining the fate of what is happening in the game. Our psyches go psycho.

Some people drown themselves in stats (ie., dads in the CCM jackets). They'll mark minutes, passes, turnovers, plus or minus, goals, assists, checks. You name it, they are counting it, and in some cases more liberally slanted to validate their own purpose in life. Or you see a videographer, perhaps for the coach or just to have something to do. Or maybe you just watch and make strange noises like "get it!" "Oh my gosh.....no" "get it out of there" "Skate skate skate beat him" "holy shit" "no no NOOOO" "AHHHH so close" "WHAT THE HELL REF... he doesn't like our team" "ooooh, that was a hard hit" "I wonder what time they went to bed, they look so sluggish" "is the ice slippier today, they keep falling" and "those other boys are mean, they are huge." The comments are the same, you revert to your habits whether it's jibber jabber or meaningful content (although compared to Pee Wee years, you are more invested in the jibber jabber).

When your team is winning, the euphoric feelings start happening IF your kid did something productive and is playing well. However, it's OKAY to acknowledge the pit in your stomach if your kid just doesn't have it that game but you need to appear happy that your team is still doing well. It's also OKAY to secretly do mental flips when your kid scored or did something amazing and they still lost. The kid may look like they are upset and you need to respect the ceremony, but it's that private text or phone call where you get to say "THAT GOAL was AWESOME, you played great!" And this way the kid can release to someone they trust.

At Nationals, there is definitely more fanfare. I assume it's similar for prep school playoffs or any other hockey final set of games like a state championship. The rink welcomes you with a balloon arch, a person checking wristbands and of course a rush hour of wet-headed hockey players zig-zagging in and out of the entrance, parents, scouts, grandparents and t-shirt vendors. Stairs going up are for the scouts who have a special cordoned-off space. No entry for parents. Advisors huddle around the prospect who just played a game. They may include parents in their conversation and suavely introduce them to a scout for a prospective team in the future. Then, they will politely excuse themselves, shaking a dad's hand and patting the player on the back. Onto the next, resembling a ritual akin to self-pollinating other prospects in the lobby. These guys don't put all their eggs in one basket, they need to have a diversified portfolio.

Just know there are so many variables that go into the equation of whether your player is approached at this stage of the process. It feels more like a mathematical formula for satellite re-entry. A complex process. At the most competitive level, every player is trained to work on the same things (skating, hockey IQ, skills, competitiveness). Goalies have a different set of must-haves, which also include a minimum man-body height of at least 6'2." For the forwards and defensemen, large statures matter. So do grades and character. While any of those three are nice-to-haves, if they dominate on something that sets them apart from everyone else, that can be their ticket.

To get noticed, and ultimately recruited, what matters is how s/he performs in the sticky situations. All of those early morning skates and off-ice work create the elite athlete. Being coachable and possessing an unwavering belief in and love of the game, even better. These kids are always working, they only make it *look* easy.

During Nationals, we won our first two games. The boys were electric and had played a team who had beaten them 3 times that season. They hit back hard, our team was in sync every step of the way. Second game, great hockey. Interesting to note that one of our goalies had lost his grandfather. He missed the first game because the family had to fly to another state, pay their respects, and mourn. Then they drove 12 hours to make the second game. The goalie played well (save percentage was .962), putting the mental skill of compartmentalizing to the test.

Third game, we lost. The boys were not making smart plays and definitely seemed to play to their own individual athleticism. This is where you just start questioning everything...the coaches choice for the power play, the messy passing, the lack of chemistry between lines. Then one of our top defensemen took a hit to the head as he was getting the puck. He was taken from the rink with a neck brace, on a stretcher. What a horrible sight for any hockey parent, watching your ghost-white kid get loaded into the ambulance. He couldn't feel his left leg, and he was dizzy, so they kept him overnight. After an MRI on his neck, they discovered that his spinal cord was bruised and he had a mild concussion. A stinger. It wasn't this kid's first concussion, so immediately the entire family goes down the rabbit hole of hockey what-ifs.

Based on round-robin and points, we were still able to advance. Nobody expected our team to get beyond their third game. We hadn't even made hotel reservations past that day. This is where all of the superstitions and rituals came out. A few of the moms decided to call themselves the hockey witches, performing all types of rituals involving chants and prayers. One mom and I decided that we could do some numerology as to where we sat, what the score was, and if we divided the number 9 we would somehow trick the hockey gods in our favor. This just made us feel better, of course. It had no actual effect.

Or did it?

At some point after the second period, we were down 3-1, so we headed outside for oxygen. Parents from the other team were gathered in a circle, in a state of euphoria. They were talking about how sweet their goals were. Our guys seemed to be getting outplayed and our optimism began to wane. My witch-hockey-mom friend and I decided their energy was bringing down our vibe, so we headed back inside. We stopped, made small talk about the team photo with some other parents, and decided we'd better sit somewhere else this time. I noticed my husband split up from his father; people were going to different rows. Some sat, some stood. The one thing I know is that the dad who was manning the penalty box when we won two of our games was back in the box, so we considered that a good sign. We picked our seats (decided that some variation of 918 was good, so we found section 118, row 9 and looked up the angel of 918). Seriously, some weird shit, but it's an effective coping mechanism when voodoo and woo-woo is all you have to offer. As the kids came out, the

AC/DC song "Thunderstruck" blared and the boys looked ready to play. No more messing around, in that game my son made an awesome assist to his linemate for a goal, then two more goals by other players (one in overtime), and we were headed to the semifinals.

Many of us parents lost our voices cheering, it truly was an epic comeback.

And that is what a hockey game does for you: it takes everything away and then throws an icy bucket of water straight at your face to make you feel completely recharged! This is not like watching your hometown pro team win a game. When a team of players grows up in front of your eyes, and all those days and weekends blend together to form this one final event together, you cherish the moment and never want it to end.

As women united in purpose, we ordered some Bloody Marys. We also noticed the same group of parents who had circled together 17 minutes ago. They were no longer enjoying the feelings of euphoria and talking about sweet goals. Now they were shaking their heads in denial.

"How could we have just let a 2 goal lead go like that?"

"We were the better team, we had it and then just shit the bed."

"This just sucks. I don't even know what to say to him when he gets out."

As a fellow parent, I could identify with every statement. So I ate my celery stick, drank my Bloody Mary and gleefully walked past them to start snapping pictures of our parents grouping in the stands for my imaginary photo book I'd never create. Those photos are trapped in cyber-heaven forever.

We made it to the Championship game that year. But then we lost to a team that was just flat-out better than us. We made ourselves feel better by stating obvious facts: two kids from Canada who were early draft picks in the OHL, a bunch of college commits, blah blah blah. Our superstition of singing Bon Jovi's Living on a Prayer and having two tequila shots before the game did not pan out. We blamed the two parents who showed up late for the last game; they must have disturbed the mojo and messed it all up. Or...or maybe we just got outplayed.

Watching the boys come out of the locker room that day was a lot more emotional for me than I expected. My husband snapped a great picture of my son taking one last skate alone on the ice as he looked down at his stick, his reflection on the glass behind him. Our kid had made a decision. I watched his teammates and their parents all hugging their sons, many tear-stained sweaty faces and weepy mothers. Regardless of what advisors, coaches and other parents said or thought of him, my son knew what his next move would be.

He was done.

14

WHAT? YOU'RE DONE?

I t's the investment you mourn.

Not just the money; hockey takes what it wants. Hockey advisors, past coaches, and even your own organization will say there are no shortcuts. "Getting to the NCAA Division I status is a long shot and pouring thousands of dollars into camps, private lessons and travel is not for the faint of heart given the odds of actually making it".[1] But most hockey families will say: it was all worth it. Even the ones that need to extend their projected retirement age; still worth it.

The competitive sport world is a business, one that depends on selling a dream to willing and financially able parents. Like any other business offering, *you* are the product. The implicit nature of investing resources into a competitive athlete is dependent on the laws of supply and demand. Any time a hockey player is drafted into the NHL, someone is doing the math on the profit margin of the team comprising player age, position, existing contracts and club growth. Whether it's a pro-team, the juniors, a prep school or college team, someone is crunching the numbers to make the business profitable. The model is basic and for the most part, predictable. Many NCAA teams have their roster set for the next two years, leaving only a few openings.

Full scholarship money is often another misnomer, depending on the program. The funnel gets really small and if you think...aaaah, we made it...think again. Players get drafted to their junior team, attend the main camp and may barely play. The coach can be impossibly tough. Players can be traded. Ivy League schools don't offer athletic scholarships. In your finest hour, it could still be grim.

As an initial investment, hockey is no different than having a large insurance payment year round. There are no guaranteed returns on the money invested, but in the event a player makes it to the next level out of youth hockey, you are happy to have paid into the system. As time passes and the passion intensifies, the investment grows along with the potential payout. That payout may not come in the form of money for college, though. So, what the heck, maybe focus on grades, since an academic scholarship is way more likely.

Essentially, you're lucky if you break even, financially speaking.

Lessons, uniforms, team dues are fixed costs, there is no reason to belabor the point that playing hockey, in and of itself, is expensive. However, every hockey family knows it's impossible to quantify the time, labor and sacrifices involving the entire family. This is a riskier investment as it involves hard costs like travel and soft costs like time and perhaps missed opportunities. Marital issues. Resentment by the siblings of the hockey player. Neglecting old friends, missing things like family get-togethers, homecoming, prom, high school football games. The emotional investment comprises at least half of the hockey portfolio because there is no way to really measure all of your feelings, the highs and lows of a season, injuries and recovery, mental state (not only player, but mom and dad).

Every relationship, whether good or bad, defines the entire hockey experience. If someone told me "it's not worth it" and warned me of every single sacrifice we'd make, I'd still do it. We're gluttons for punishment, I guess. Plus, hockey is frickin' awesome!

There is a point in the hockey season where every parent is ready for a break, it's as if we've been holding our breath for 6 months. This first hits you before Christmas and you can't wait to take a break. Then it sucker punches you in the stomach by the end of February. You're fatter, you're tired, and you're emotionally hungover. Even those with kids who've committed to college still live in fear of a disabling injury or a coaching change.

I remember casual conversations in the lobby of the ice rink after a game. Hockey parents are pros at repression. We all have various protective mechanisms for hockey-induced anxiety. Much like Wall Street jitters when the Feds come out with the jobs report, so do the parents rationalize the exit strategy from the massive investment:

- "Yeah, my older son quit when he was 16; played for his high school."
- "He can't get another concussion."
- "He's much better at lacrosse and this way he can go straight to college."
- "He really should be an engineer or a doctor, I don't know if a kinesiology degree is going to pay the bills if this doesn't work out."
- "He'll never be taller than 5'7" so what's the point?"
- "All roads lead to the beer league, that's where he's headed."

After the first few years of it, I never really thought about my son *not* playing hockey. As we watched him start "late" and devote every waking moment to the sport, we were impressed by his rapid development and personal drive. We certainly believed he could achieve his goals. He had a plan, and with practice, support and perseverance, it seemed likely he'd eventually play D1 hockey. Plenty of people outside our circle of supporters said as much, scouting reports would remark at his high hockey IQ, his shot and ability to play the game "the way it's supposed to be played." We saved the emails, texts and phone calls from interested coaches and teams. He had a hockey advisor, had looked at prep schools and had a remarkable record within a highly competitive league.

However, he had been sharing his doubts with teammates and started to drop little hints throughout the season:

- "It feels like a job."
- "I don't want to live my senior year of high school in the middle of nowhere."
- "For me, it's ALL-IN or nothing, there is no in-between."
- "I don't know if I want to be 21 when I start college."
- "I have zero interest in becoming a scout, a trainer, or a kid's hockey coach."
- "I don't want to end up with CTE from too many hits to the head."
- "I want to have a normal senior year. I've never been to any dances or football games."
- "I have no free time to just hang out with friends outside of hockey."
- "I love golf. I mean, I *really* love golf."

As parents, we could've used some grief counseling; we weren't prepared for any of it. My husband and I grieved the loss of our own personal interest in enjoying the "wins" of hockey parenting. We got used to junipers. Never saw it coming from those days at the YMCA. My son's comments were sprinkled in, throughout various conversations, like breadcrumbs leading to a dream-furnace coated in candy. We alternated between "We support your decision; if you don't have the passion, it's not worth it," to "Are you *SURE*?"

We journeyed through all five stages of grief, as demonstrated by these actual quotes from my husband:

Stage One: Denial

"Don't be silly, you just need a few weeks off to relax."

"Are you sure? I don't think you're thinking through it all, it's what they call burnout. Everyone goes through that in life."

Stage Two: Anger

"WE JUST SPENT THE EQUIVALENT OF 4 YEARS OF COLLEGE ON THIS SPORT."

"There is no college money account."

"UH..... We could have gone on a nicer vacation instead of Detroit."

Stage Three: Bargaining

"Please, just give it one month, see if you miss it."

"Maybe better to play for a different coach in a different state."

Stage Four: Depression

"I could have retired earlier. Shitballs."

"I'm going to miss watching him play."

"Fuckin' Covid."

"I can't even watch hockey anymore, it makes me so sad."

Stage Five: Acceptance

"Wash the gear and put it somewhere."

"You need to take down the garage setup so I can park my car in the garage again."

"$15,000 or more on sticks in the past 6 years at $275 a pop. Can we make a nice bench from the broken sticks?"

"Wait, you're beating me at golf? You shot a 68? I've played this my entire life. You little shit."

"Nope, you need to buy your own golf putter. I am not paying for one more thing related to a sport you think you're good at. I don't care if you could have been the next Phil Mickelson, get yourself a job and pay for your own shit. I want to retire."

It was a crazy cocktail of emotions. Definitely some regrets at how we guided his choices, one of which would have been to play up in his U15 year or move teams. Maybe we should have pushed a move to a prep school sooner. A good coach who believes in your kid and helps them thrive is essential. Staying with the same team out of fear of repercussions for being disloyal is stupid. We should have moved on and had more variety of teammates to play with so skills/roles were not pigeonholed.

The Covid year rocked his plans. We woulda coulda shoulda, but who knows if any of those avenues would have panned out. Maybe the lightswitch moment of "I'm done" had nothing to do with any of that.

Navigation Tip: Woulda-coulda-shouldas will drive you nucking futs if you let them. You'll beat yourself up, question the decision points, question the value of the hockey advisor, question the worth of a coach or organization. Questioning is part of the process of letting go. You can't change the past and despite your best efforts to encourage the endurance through the rough spots, it's not really your path to climb once they've made their decision to stop. Let them find a new path to a different mountain, they can handle the extra weight now.

One thing I know is that the salty nature of a hockey team is like a layer of sunscreen for life. It protects them from the harmful rays of adversity in the next challenge. Camaraderie, team work, chirps and immunity from insults - all of it builds resilience. Anytime they feel inadequate on the ice, they push themselves to get past it. This type of drive is a skill that serves them well off the ice. I'd venture to guess it's the same in other competitive sports.

While on a team, they have a sense of purpose. To juggle their sport and school and strive to get to the next level provides the stepping stones for a hard work ethic. If you want something bad enough, you have to put the work into it regardless of whether the dream is realized in the end. It's the growth mindset, I know because it's what got me through 3 years of law school and two bar exams.

Passion for the game. Talent. Grit. Perseverance. Endurance. All of these are attributes of a competitive athlete with the x-factor of an "all-in" mentality.

Once my husband and I got through our grieving period, we decided to focus our efforts on supporting him in his rebranding process. Most of these kids have been described as a "hockey player" for so long that their identities are wrapped up in it; deciding to do something else seems overwhelming. I had a friend who was a competitive gymnast all the way through college. When it was over, she was clinically depressed. She didn't know what to do with the 30+ hours of gym time that was now hers. Her friends were all gymnasts and her life had revolved around her sport.

When the season ended, my son slowly started to talk about life plans. The good habits (fitness and nutrition) stayed with him all summer. Where it got tricky was the sudden influx of a commodity he was not at all used to: free time. I swear he spent more time laying on the couch that summer than he had his entire life. Drudgery ensued as we insisted he do more chores around the house and focus on finding a summer job. We joked that "maybe playing hockey is better."

Three months later, he was happier. Lighter. Less stressed. We were also less stressed as the cancerous pit of hockey despair went into remission. He was working, spending more time with his girlfriend and the friends he had managed to keep throughout high school. He was still in touch with his hockey team, exchanging jabs and updates as if nothing had changed. We found someone to work with him on a college search, which thankfully helped him understand his own interests and strengths. Meanwhile, I was off in the corner with one eye shut, smoking cigarettes and rocking back and forth mumbling to myself. Just kidding, I had tenants in Oklahoma who were trying to just survive. Perspective.

It all worked out, in the end.

When I started writing this book, it was therapy. Cathartic. I had so many emotions that I couldn't quite reign in, unlike any other time in my life. My own personal challenges seemed like little mountains next to this, and I enjoy climbing actual mountains.

My older sons played sports, but they did them at recreational or high school athletic programs. I knew they enjoyed it, it was fun to watch them play, and that was enough. Their extracurricular passions were diversified - skiing, hiking, girls, parties, friends.

My youngest daughter excelled at competitive dance, but after watching a few episodes of Dance Moms together, we both decided that was bullshit for the long haul and diversified with other interests.

With hockey, I could see it was a treacherous route but eventually got behind the notion that our kid could get there. His "there" was originally the NHL. Then, more realistically, juniors and maybe a DI college.

I had watched sports specials about Olympic athletes who worked full time jobs and got up at 4 am to practice. How they overcame injury and waited another 4 years for their one shot. It was those stories of average athletes, underdogs, and those that were underestimated that I've always enjoyed. I thought of the early morning skates I'd take him to, tearing up when his skates were the first marks on the fresh ice.

We were not a hockey family, in the beginning. We were not genetically gifted although we have one son who was 6 feet tall. We didn't know anyone who played the sport. We sacrificed a lot of money, time and mental health to help our third kid go for it. We mourned when it was over. But we have healed.

How many times as a parent do you review the dreams you had as a kid? Did you actually achieve everything you dreamed your life would be? Did you try?

It's the journey, not the destination.

As a latch-key kid in the '80s, everyone in my circle was on their own when it came to deciphering plans after high school. Going to college was considered a luxury in my neck of the woods. I had a blue-collar upbringing where most kids were encouraged to go into the trades or find a job locally. I remember the school counselor just smirking at me when I said I wanted to be a doctor. Then a lawyer. Then a forest ranger. I was able to put myself through law school, then ended up changing careers 5 times.

I am so proud of my son for getting as far as he did. He truly was fun to watch over the years and I should thank him for entertaining us. He could have been a blob on the couch who smoked pot and had a bad attitude. But hockey prevented that version of him, if it existed. Instead, I have a kid who "retired" from something he believed he had taken to its furthest point. Once it wasn't fun and the passion was waning, it became a mirror for any bad relationship. Yes, he could have attempted to push past it and found inspiration elsewhere, but he chose to trust his gut. It wasn't about work ethic at that point, it was about intuition and logic. His sense of humor was formed by the very nature of being around driven athletes who pushed each other down just as hard as they lifted each other up. It truly was a magical phenomena that I know he will treasure as the years go by.

Navigation Tip: When it's time to get off the hamster wheel, seek out the parents whose kids moved on as well. They will console you, because the grief is real unless you really hated the sport and sacrifices anyway. There's just as much to learn from people who don't summit the mountain, but it does feel like sending your horse out to pasture. Going to high school to be a "normal" kid is an adjustment. Eating together as a family is weird.

I like to see him post the successes of his teammates on social media. It's wonderful to see how most of his teammates are progressing to the next level in hockey. Even the formerly-jealous-WTF version of me has disappeared. I don't miss the stress and 3 a.m. anxiety-driven sleep disorders. I now have a piece of myself back that was in hockey-parent-worry-purgatory. The emotional roller-coaster is gone, I have a life again. The juniper plant stopped getting the sun it needed to thrive, so it died. Battles of the "wins" and the "successes" of all of those events compared to the dread and the despair are gone now, happy memories for the rest.

As for anyone who's played a competitive sport, the lessons learned and discipline and drive will make your athlete successful in life. I'm sure there will be a few that need counseling if they left because of injury or other type of abuse, but for the most part it creates some pretty kick-ass people.

Ever watch NHL hockey players give TV interviews? They attribute all of their success to the team, their coach and support from their families. If they make a mistake, they acknowledge it and accept the loss. They never blame the refs in public. They don't throw teammates under the bus. They stick to what they need to do better. They train, they practice and they learn from mistakes. Even if they get injured, they get right back on the ice. They can take a puck to the face and barely flinch, only addressing it because the trainer can't have blood dripping on the ice. Does this mean they don't feel pain? No. Of course they feel pain. They choose not to let it control them.

They are responsible, driven, disciplined and humble. Their fitness, diet and attention to rest and recovery is nurtured by years of habit. They are good friends to have, they are witty, quick with the chirps, and have a tendency to be good at anything they decide to pursue once they leave the sport.

I have more perspective than I did then. It took time to reflect and digest all of that stress in order to see that you can only guide, not climb the climb for your player. It is their mindset, shaped by so many external factors that deep in their soul will tell them how far they need to dig deep to keep playing. Love, passion, grit, skill and hard work is only part of it. The rest is up to them.

15

OVERTIME

Never gloat about a two-goal lead in hockey until you hear the final buzzer.

We're going to overtime.

The players can feel every second on the ice. The adage of "practice how you play" is the basis for every pass, every shot attempt, every block, every save. True grit. Palpable energy. Dialed in. The goalie looks like Godzilla hitting small planes out of the sky. Spectators, especially the goalie parents, stop breathing only to exhale by mumbling Aramaic verses to themselves. There is a layer of excitement mixed with dread in the bleachers, prayers and superstitions in full force.

Meanwhile, the kids are absolutely fine; this is fun for them. The music between whistles seems louder, more intense. A little AC/DC, some Jump Around from House of Pain, maybe an original version of Eye of the Tiger. You name it, hockey playlists rock (if you have the right DJ). The moms start seat-dancing to work off the jitters. Look around the stands, there's a dad up there doing a mini-headbang to TNT or Kickstart my Heart. It's awesome.

Coaches scribble plays on their whiteboards, players listen to every word. A good coach can change a game, but a great coach can change a life. Ok, now I do BELIEVE in Ted Lasso shit, it *is* real life. At this moment, all you're thinking about is the game. Lines roll, some get passed over. It is time to win this game. They want to win. It's fun to win.

You take pleasure when the other team misses their shots; even better if they go in the box. Haters gonna hate, parents gonna celebrate. Sorry kid, it's hockey. A game of mistakes and schadenfreude.

Since the Romans built the Colosseum in 80 A.D., humans have loved gladiators. We're drawn to them. Next time you watch a hockey game, slow down the video when there's a good hit or fight. Thank goodness these guys don't have spears on the end of their sticks. We love it all (unless your kid gets knocked out cold, then not so much).

Picture every motivational poster out there. It all applies in OT. You suddenly remember the first time your kid picked out their new hockey stick. How they stickhandled with a lacrosse ball in the store, assessing the flex and choosing the one that felt the best in their hands. My kid would bring it home and sleep with it until it became the back up stick he'd bring to tournaments after about 2 months. Sticks are slutty that way.

I did not know I was capable of such epic mood swings. In one minute, I would be furious, having a dialogue with myself of complete vitriol that could be completely wiped away if my kid scored a goal. What is that? I could hold my breath for entire shifts while feeling my heart beat in my temples. I could be laughing one minute and dead silent the second my kid stepped on the ice or was passed over for his shift.

It was addictive. And then it was over. No, it didn't go to a shootout. It was just over...sort of.

Remember I told you my son was done with hockey? Well, my husband and I talked him into playing for his high school in his senior year so we could watch him play. Our denial stage was a little longer than expected. It was methadone for our 6 years of addiction to the hockey opiate. He had a great high school golf season and was applying to colleges, all good. He joined the hockey team, knocking some hopeful kids down in the roster. It felt like a favor to us, as we were the ones who needed closure. The coaches were thrilled to have him. He agreed, though his heart wasn't in it, as he'd left it on the ice with his team at Nationals.

Bob Dylan once said, "Take care of all your memories. For you cannot relive them." I wish I had been better at organizing the video I had captured on my phone, or pictures I had taken over the course of his hockey career. Damn iCloud abyss.

Unlike Minnesota, high school hockey in the west is a little chippy. For us, it was like watching a washed up Broadway star end up in a community production of A Chorus Line. Like keeping your old dog alive with meds, just not quite ready to euthanize our spectatorship. It was more like Pet Cemetery: it died, and we tried to revive it. But it wasn't the same. Not even close. He went to all the workouts, practices, team scrimmages and games. He "performed" where he could, but much of the team's skill set resembled where he was at the age of 14. The parents were sweet, the players were nice. End of the season, he made us laugh when describing how he felt when they lost in the play-offs. He had to put his shirt over his mouth and look at the floor, feigning being "sad" about being done with hockey as the others who had played their last high school game openly wept and hugged. They were definitely heading for gap years or college next. The coaches encouraged our son to keep going, as they were hockey guys. One coach insisted he played like Cole Caulfield. Both were Minnesota born, say no more. It was in their blood.

Our son was a hockey widower, encouraged to "date" hockey again as a high school senior.

But you know what was really cool? The high school had loud student cheering sections, posters, Senior night presentations, memorabilia, girlfriends watching, girlfriend's parents watching. A real hometown game. Must be what it feels like to play high school hockey in Minnesota.

For the first time in years, we were there for the hockey.

There were no scouts, no pressure to succeed beyond the game.

The music playlist was fabulous and well thought out. Kids cheered for the biggest hits and ooohed and ahhhhhd at his skating moves, weaving in and out, deking the goalie, skating complete circles looking for someone to pass. It was quite comical, like the SNL skit where Payton Manning is playing football with middle-schoolers and tells them they suck as he nails a kid in the chest with the ball. Not that my kid racked up the points that season, it's a team sport. But there were moments - much like when an old dog perks up and chases the rabbit - that I could see his old hockey self, the one that was having fun. Just fun. It was those moments in the stands that brought me to tears! I would look over at my husband with a proud nod. He would chug his beer to hide his tears of joy. I'd send him a text, "I'm not crying, you're crying."

So when your player quits, gets injured or cut from teams too many times, it's not the end of the world. The kids are alright. Life goes on.

I loved the experience, and now I'm rooting for the boys who are still living the hockey dream - even if it's in a league that gets them to club hockey or a later hockey coach role. I have walked through the pearly gates and submitted to the afterlife of hockey. I watch hockey without being sad. I'm excited to see the Stanley Cup playoffs. I can't wait to see those that make it to the next level, to plan a trip to watch the others play. When one of them gets married, to get to "party" with the whole group again. Fandango Part II. I love the get-togethers with moms at cabins or for a movie or a hike. We are the veterans who have lived through, and in, something that was magical and is no longer ulcer-producing. Never underestimate the power of those relationships.

Today, my husband and I laugh at how we used to email each other with what we wanted to say to the coach, especially the last year of AAA. It would start with, "Should we say something?" as the writing prompt for the reply, "NO...DO NOT SEND." The 3 a.m. thoughts would brew and affect our sleep, but we always let it go wide, much like the puck when it misses an empty net.

Allow me to be complicit in your mania. Need that scream pillow?

A good kickboxing class? Some Tito's? Whatever it is, always pause and breathe, the kid will decide what they need to do next if presented with realistic options. Give them some credit, they are smarter than we treat them sometimes. They develop poise. The stress and desire to interfere or control the outcome is futile. Podcasts and coaches tell us "The parents are crazy" when... well.... we are. *Sometimes*. However, it's an environment full of fear-based propaganda. Remember, it is an industry. Much of it is for profit. It is not always a level playing field. It beats you down, tells you not to say the wrong thing, do the wrong thing, and whatever you do, don't be *THAT* parent. Heck, it's advice I've shared in this very book, I was brainwashed like everyone else.

It is difficult to prepare for how your player will handle the stressors. Sometimes you see your player hurting inside. You see them retreat. Look sad. Ignore requests to talk about it. Then they pick up their stick, and go out again. They are resilient. They are trying to figure it out. Just keep encouraging them to work at it, rather than chiding them for not working hard enough.

You will tire of all the catchphrases and clichés as the kid gets older. It's not one size fits all, despite the posters with slogans over the locker room doors. Sometimes hockey coaches diagnose the lagging player by applying the cliché, and think that's going to explain away all of the hours spent practicing, mentally preparing, the sacrifices made in order to play the sport, without really tuning into the player's mindset in the moment. They may be thinking: Keep your head up. Keep your stick on the ice. Shoot the puck on net. Don't let your teammates down. Don't let your parents down.

Just remember:

 "Rowing harder doesn't help if the boat is headed in the wrong direction."

— Kenichi Ohmae

And then you recall all the good times. They go by so fast. Nostalgic moments will emerge, maybe the next time you check into a hotel, seeing a team of Pee Wees awkwardly dropping their bags in the lobby, kids playing knee hockey in the halls, or seeing hockey parents spill out of a pizza restaurant with a gaggle of sweaty kids. You notice the drywall of your garage, riddled with holes, or find an errant puck in the corner-most spot of a shelf. Old jerseys stuffed in the back of the closet, a worn out hat, a bag of green biscuits neatly settled in a spot near the camping equipment.

You're fine. They're fine.
    God Bless Hockey.

STICK TAPS

So many people to thank...

Let's start with the inspiration, the hockey parents. I am so thankful for the friendships. Grateful for the hours of conversations in the bleachers, the lobbies, the cars, the planes, and the coffee shops. I hit the jackpot with you. Hap and Jodi, Michelle and Mike, Monica and Andy, Vlad and Victoria, Milan and Zlata, Sasha and Irene, Rob and Kourtney, Pat and Lisa, Chrissy and Mike, Jim and Kim, Bret and Kellie, Rob, Kellie, Wendi and Rob, Peter and Holly, Jackson and Sandi, John, Matt, Melissa, Katie, Brian and Kelli, Scott and Tracey, Susan and Jim, Carmen and James, Julie and Chris, Megan and Aaron, Melania and Piotr, Brian and Rachel, Shelley, Hugh and Anyes, Ryan-Randy and Elise, Nichelle and Kris, Susan and Doug, Mendi and Warren, Jim and Liz, Ashley, Nikki and Heather.

The true gentlemen who nurtured the hockey embryo, thank you for your dedication and willingness to share your knowledge and expertise:

Tim Naiman, Chris Morgan, Tony Zurn, Stephen Cunningham, Matt Schoepflin, Peter Senja.

Pavel, Lukas and Grapes.

In memory of Sergei Bautin.

To my four children, there is nothing that makes me happier than seeing you all thrive. Let nothing dim the light that shines from within. I am so lucky you are mine. I love you.

To my sister, Nancy Pienkowski. Your humor and editing advice had me laughing so much, you could have been a hockey player. Chicago humor is a great baseline for satire.

To my brother, John Pienkowski, thank you for sharing your stories about facing adversity from your time serving as Commanding Officer in the U.S. Navy. Your motivational humor, application of Star Wars quotes, and prayers always came in handy. Embrace the suck.

To my parents and in-laws, I am so thankful to have such a caring and compassionate family who I can always count on. No words can properly convey the respect and love I have for you. To my father, for his mantras throughout my life, "Carpe Diem" and "Don't let the bastards wear you down."

To Kristi and Mike. To Steve. For opening my eyes to an entire world of blessed hearts, hard work and friendship.

To the sisterhood of our writing group, Tami Palmer, Kim Kleeman, Allyn Harker, Jessica Goldmuntz Stokes, Elena Davis, Esther Cohen and Suzanne Strobel. I will always cherish the retreats and honor the writing muse that was summoned in Glenwood Springs. I am so grateful for your friendship, feedback and coaching.

To the wonderful authors and writers at Red Thread Publishing, thank you for welcoming me into your community.

To my writing partner, Gill Tillman, my Canadian counterpart who kept me on track in the final stretch.

To my husband, Jamie. You are my rock. You always know how to make me laugh. You tried to warn me about the hockey thing, but even you got sucked in. Thank you – these two little words carry all my respect, love, and gratefulness for you and for all that you do to make my life better.

And finally, to my hockey son. I would do it all again in a heartbeat. Thanks for being such a good kid and making me laugh every day. Hockey hockey hockey hockey hockey.

ABOUT THE AUTHOR

Laura Zukosky is a writer, mother of four and master of the side-hustle. Her starring role as a Hockey Team Manager in the book is one of multiple identities during her time as a hockey parent. On a quest to squeeze every possible bit of enjoyment out of life, she lives in Colorado with her spirit animal - a long-haired German Shepherd dog named Koda. She also has another dog, Taser, named after the pro-hockey player Jonathan Towes who is way too serious. Besides dogs, she lives with her husband Jamie and teenage daughter who is a reluctant only child as her three brothers flew the coop to pursue their own talents and dreams. She hopes this book will get her invited to the VIP box for Chicago Blackhawks games, perhaps a dinner with Eddie Olczyk.

YOUR REVIEW MATTERS

If you enjoyed this book or found it helpful, we would greatly appreciate a simple review. It only takes one minute.

Amazon amzn.to/3ZJG2fE

or on **GoodReads.**

Scan the code to get directly to the Amazon review page.

ABOUT THE PUBLISHER
RED THREAD BOOKS

Red Thread Publishing is an all-female publishing company on a mission to support 10,000 women to become successful published authorpreneurs & thought leaders.

To work with us or connect regarding any of our growing library of books email us at **info@redthreadbooks.com.**
 To learn more bout us visit our website **www.redthreadbooks.com.**

Follow us & join the community.

f facebook.com/redthreadpublishing
◎ instagram.com/redthreadbooks

NOTES

2. The Hook and Reel

1. Flanagan, L. (2022). *Take back the game: How money and mania are ruining kids' sports--and why it matters.* Portfolio / Penguin, an imprint of Penguin Random House LLC.

3. Crossing the Rubicon

1. Small area games are drills done in small areas like the corners or cross-ice. I'm not a coach, but there are plenty of ways a good one can develop individual and team skills.

5. The Off-Season Money Pit

1. United States Hockey League, considered the top junior ice hockey league by USA Hockey.
2. North American Hockey League, considered Tier 2 junior league, sends players to NCAA Division 1.
3. Western Hockey League, considered a major junior hockey league in Western Canada and the Northwest part of the USA. Players cannot play Division 1 Hockey if they play in this league.

6. Arrested Development

1. Wikimedia Foundation. (2022, November 2). *Arrested development.* Wikipedia. Retrieved January 18, 2023, from https://en.wikipedia.org/wiki/Arrested_development

7. The Parent Fandango

1. British Columbia Hockey League is a Junior A ice league under Hockey Canada. Players are allowed to play in college if they advance.
2. National Collegiate Athletic Association.

8. The Rinks and the Rats

1. Wikimedia Foundation. (2022, May 30). *Flehmen response*. Wikipedia. Retrieved January 18, 2023, from https://en.wikipedia.org/wiki/Flehmen_response

12. Broken Sticks

1. https://uscenterforsafesport.org/

14. What? You're done?

1. Great article describing the odds, *Do your homework & maximize the odds.* Kreezee Sports. (n.d.). Retrieved January 18, 2023, from https://www.dmvhockeyprospects.com/news/do-your-homework-maximize-the-odds-38370

Made in the USA
Coppell, TX
03 April 2023

15176210R00121